Business Ethics

ISBN: 9798224733606

License Notes

This book remains the copyrighted property of the author, and no part of this book may be reproduced, stored in or introduced into a retrieval system, or transmitted, in any form, or by any means (electronic, mechanical, photocopying, recording or otherwise) without the prior written permission of the author. Any person who commits an unauthorized act in relation to this book can be liable to criminal prosecution and civil claims for damages. If you like this book, please encourage your friends to buy their own copy from their favorite authorized retailer.

We appreciate your suggestions & support.

Disclaimer:-

"This book is strictly based on syllabus of prescribed by Savitribai Phule Pune University for autonomous and non-autonomous college. This book is not claiming any right on any information used from previous research and books. That information is used only as reference for additional knowledge. All efforts have been made to make it error free, but if any mistakes or errors are found feel free to mail us on following email-ID for improvements. We always accept your valuable suggestions.

e-mail: hmrspoetry@gmail.com

Table of Contents

Acknowledgment

This book would not have been possible without the help of many amazing people.

To my parents, who taught me the importance of hard work and dedication.

To almighty Lord for his intangible presence at every stage of life.

To my teachers (Mrs. Sudha, Mrs. Saroj Bala, Mrs. Ranjana Bhatnagar, Mrs. Anupama Gupta,

Mrs. Mamta) and mentors (Dr. M. D. Lawrence & Mr. D. K. Sharma) who helped me along the

way.

To my wife, for her moral support.

To my students (Ashu, Disha, Tarun, Ashish, Mansi, Jyoti, Sayali, Khushi, Vaibhavi, Akshada, Krishna, Garv, Krish, Ansh, Siddhant, Yashavi, and all regular students of TY_BBA_SP_College)

who kept me inspired and motivated even when I wanted to give up.

To my colleagues (Mrs. Gauri Jadhav, Mrs. Shilpa Khade, Mrs. Archana Mhaske, Mrs.

Tejashree Tawre, Ms. Heena Shaikh, Mr. Armaan Shaikh, Mrs. Pinkle Doshi, who offered

support and encouragement.

To Ajit, who act as guide to write regularly.

And to the readers, who will make this book a success.

Thank you all for making this dream, a reality.

Chapter 1. Introduction to Business Ethics

1.1 Meaning, Nature and Scope of Business Ethics

1.2 Ethics in Contemporary Business

1.3 Organizational Ethical Climate – Ethical Decision Making and Importance of Framing Ethical Policies

1.4Why Ethical Problems occur in Business

1.5 Difference between workplace Ethics and Laws

1.6 Ethical Code of Conduct in Global Business

1.7 Government protection policies against illegal business practices.

1.8 Influence of Interest Groups on the Government

1.1 Meaning, Nature and Scope of Business Ethics

The history of ethics can be traced back to the ancient world, with the earliest recorded discussions of ethics found in the writings of the ancient Greeks. The Greek philosophers Socrates, Plato, and Aristotle all made significant contributions to the development of ethical thought.

Socrates (469-399 BCE) was the first Greek philosopher to focus on ethics. He believed that the key to living a good life was to know what is good and to act accordingly. He developed a method of inquiry called the Socratic method, which involved questioning people's beliefs in order to help them to discover their own ignorance.

Plato (428-348 BCE) was a student of Socrates, and he developed his teacher's ideas in his own writings. Plato believed that there is an objective standard of good and evil, and that this standard is accessible to reason. He argued that the goal of ethics is to achieve eudaimonia, which is often translated as "happiness" or "flourishing."

Aristotle (384-322 BCE) was a student of Plato, and he further developed his teacher's ideas in his own writings. Aristotle believed that ethics is about practical wisdom, or the ability to make good decisions in the context of everyday life. He argued that the goal of ethics is to achieve eudaimonia, which he defined as "activity of the soul in accordance with virtue."

Ethics:

A Greek word that means "character" or "custom." It is often used to refer to the moral character of a person or organization.

Ethos:

A Greek word that means "character" or "custom." It is often used to refer to the moral character of a person or organization.

Values:

The beliefs and principles that are important to us. They guide our behavior and help us to make decisions.

Morality:

A system of beliefs about right and wrong. It is often based on religious or cultural values.

1.1.1. The Background of Business Ethics

The background of business ethics can be traced back to the early days of commerce, when merchants and traders began to develop codes of conduct to govern their interactions with each other. These early codes of conduct were often based on religious or moral principles, and they emphasized the importance of honesty, fairness, and trustworthiness.

In the 19th century, the Industrial Revolution led to a number of new ethical challenges for businesses. As businesses grew in size and complexity, they began to have a greater impact on society. This led to a growing awareness of the need for businesses to act ethically, and a number of new ethical theories were developed to guide business decision-making.

In the 20th century, the rise of multinational corporations led to even more complex ethical challenges. Businesses that operate in multiple countries are faced with a variety of different ethical standards, and they must often make difficult decisions about how to balance the interests of different stakeholders.

In recent years, there has been a growing focus on the importance of business ethics. This is due in part to a number of high-profile corporate scandals, which have highlighted the need for businesses to act ethically. It is also due to the increasing globalization of business, which has made it more important for businesses to be aware of the ethical standards of different cultures.

1.1.2. Nature of Business Ethics

The nature of business ethics is a complex and evolving topic. However, there are some key principles that can be identified.

First, business ethics is based on the idea that there are moral standards that apply to business conduct. These standards are not always clear-cut, and there may be different interpretations of what is ethical in different situations. However, there are some general principles that can be agreed upon, such as the importance of honesty, fairness, and respect for others.

Second, business ethics is concerned with the impact of business on society. Businesses have a responsibility to act in a way that is beneficial to society as a whole, and not just to their own shareholders or employees. This means taking into account the environmental impact of business activities, as well as the social impact on employees, customers, and other stakeholders.

Third, business ethics is about making difficult decisions. There will often be situations where there is no clear-cut ethical answer, and businesses will need to weigh the different factors involved in order to make the best decision. This requires businesses to have a strong ethical framework in place, as well as the ability to make ethical decisions in a timely and effective manner.

The nature of business ethics is a complex and evolving topic. However, the principles outlined above provide a good starting point for understanding what business ethics is all about.

1.1.3. Scope of Business Ethics

Business ethics is a broad and complex field that encompasses a wide range of topics. Some of the key areas of business ethics include corporate governance, accountability, fairness, transparency, and social responsibility.

- **Corporate governance** is the system by which businesses are controlled and directed. It is concerned with ensuring that businesses are managed in a responsible and ethical manner.
- **Accountability** is the responsibility that businesses have to their stakeholders, such as shareholders, employees, customers, and the community. It is about ensuring that businesses are transparent about their activities and that they are held accountable for their actions.
- **Fairness** is the principle that businesses should treat all

stakeholders fairly, regardless of their race, gender, religion, or sexual orientation. It is about ensuring that businesses do not discriminate against any group of people.

- **Transparency** is the principle that businesses should be open and honest about their activities. It is about ensuring that businesses are willing to share information with their stakeholders and that they are not trying to hide anything.

- **Social responsibility** is the principle that businesses have a responsibility to act in a way that is beneficial to society as a whole. It is about ensuring that businesses take into account the social and environmental impact of their activities.

These are just some of the key areas of business ethics. The scope of business ethics is constantly evolving, as new ethical challenges emerge and as businesses become more globalized. However, the principles outlined above provide a good starting point for understanding what business ethics is all about.

1.2. Ethics in Contemporary Business

Ethics in contemporary business is a complex and ever-evolving field. Businesses are increasingly faced with ethical challenges, as they operate in a globalized and interconnected world. These challenges can range from issues of corporate governance and social responsibility to the ethical implications of new technologies.

There are a number of factors that have contributed to the growing importance of ethics in contemporary business. These include:

- The increasing globalization of business. As businesses operate in more and more countries, they are exposed to different cultures and ethical standards. This can make it difficult to navigate ethical challenges.

- The rise of new technologies. New technologies, such as artificial intelligence and social media, have raised new ethical concerns. For example, businesses need to be careful about how they use data collected from their customers, and they need to be mindful of the potential for social media to be used to spread misinformation.
- The increasing awareness of corporate social responsibility. Businesses are increasingly being held accountable for their social and environmental impact. This has led to a growing focus on corporate social responsibility (CSR), which is the idea that businesses have a responsibility to act in a way that is beneficial to society as a whole.

There are a number of different approaches to ethics in contemporary business. Some businesses adopt a "deontological" approach, which focuses on following a set of ethical principles, such as honesty and fairness. Other businesses adopt a "utilitarian" approach, which focuses on making decisions that produce the greatest good for the greatest number of people. Still other businesses adopt a "virtue ethics" approach, which focuses on developing the virtues, such as courage and compassion, that are necessary for ethical decision-making.

1.2.2. Importance of Contemporary Business Ethics

Some of the reasons why contemporary business ethics is important:

- **It can help businesses to avoid legal problems.** Businesses that engage in unethical behavior can be subject to legal penalties, such as fines, lawsuits, and even criminal charges. By following ethical principles, businesses can help to protect themselves from these risks.
- **It can help businesses to build trust with their stakeholders.** Stakeholders, such as customers, employees,

investors, and the community, are more likely to do business with businesses that they trust. By behaving ethically, businesses can build trust with their stakeholders and create a positive reputation.

- **It can help businesses to attract and retain top talent.** Employees are more likely to want to work for businesses that they believe are ethical. By behaving ethically, businesses can attract and retain top talent, which can give them a competitive advantage.
- **It can help businesses to operate more effectively.** Businesses that behave ethically are more likely to have a positive work environment, which can lead to increased productivity and innovation.
- **It can help businesses to contribute to society.** Businesses that behave ethically can help to make the world a better place. For example, businesses can contribute to social welfare by providing jobs, donating to charity, and supporting environmental protection.

- **Increased profits:** Businesses that behave ethically are more likely to have happy customers and employees, which can lead to increased profits.
- **Improved reputation:** Businesses that behave ethically are more likely to have a positive reputation, which can attract new customers and investors.
- **Reduced risk:** Businesses that behave ethically are less likely to be involved in scandals or legal problems, which can reduce their risk.
- **Enhanced employee morale:** Employees who work for ethical businesses are more likely to be satisfied with their jobs, which can lead to increased morale and productivity.

- **Improved decision-making:** Businesses that have a strong ethical culture are more likely to make sound decisions that are in the best interests of all stakeholders.

Overall, there are many good reasons why businesses should focus on ethics. By behaving ethically, businesses can improve their bottom line, their reputation, and their overall performance.

1.3. Organizational Ethical Climate:

The ethical climate of an organization is the moral atmosphere of the workplace and the level of ethics that are practiced within the company. It is a set of shared perceptions of the procedures and policies, both formal and informal, that shape expectations for ethical behavior within an organization.

There are five main types of organizational ethical climate:

- **Instrumental climate:** This climate emphasizes the importance of achieving results, even if it means bending or breaking the rules.
- **Caring climate:** This climate emphasizes the importance of treating others with respect and compassion, even if it means sacrificing some profits.
- **Law and order climate:** This climate emphasizes the importance of following the rules, even if it means sacrificing some flexibility.
- **Rules climate:** This climate emphasizes the importance of following the rules, even if it means sacrificing some creativity.
- **Independence climate:** This climate emphasizes the importance of individual freedom and autonomy, even if it means making decisions that are not in the best interests of

the organization.

The type of organizational ethical climate that exists in a company can have a significant impact on the behavior of employees. For example, in a company with an instrumental ethical climate, employees are more likely to engage in unethical behavior if they believe it will help them achieve their goals. On the other hand, in a company with a caring ethical climate, employees are more likely to engage in ethical behavior even if it means sacrificing some profits.

1.3.1. Decision Making Process

Decision making is the process of making choices by identifying a decision, gathering information, and evaluating alternative solutions. It is a complex process that involves a number of different steps.

The process of decision making can be divided into the following steps:

1. **Identify the decision:** The first step is to identify the decision that needs to be made. What is the problem that needs to be solved? What is the question that needs to be answered?
2. **Gather relevant information:** Once you have identified the decision, you need to gather relevant information. This information can come from a variety of sources, such as your own experience, research, and the advice of others.
3. **Identify the alternatives:** Once you have gathered relevant information, you need to identify the alternatives. What are the different courses of action that you could take?
4. **Weigh the evidence:** Once you have identified the alternatives, you need to weigh the evidence. What are the pros and cons of each alternative?
5. **Choose among alternatives:** Once you have weighed the evidence, you need to choose among the alternatives. What is

the best course of action?

6. **Take action:** Once you have made a decision, you need to take action. This means implementing your decision and following through on your plan.

7. **Review your decision:** After you have taken action, you need to review your decision. Did you make the right decision? What could you have done differently?

The process of decision making is not always linear. You may need to go back and forth between the different steps as you gather more information and weigh the evidence. However, following these steps can help you make more informed and deliberate decisions.

1.3.2. Importance of Framing Ethical Policies

Framing ethical policies is the process of defining and communicating the ethical values and principles that guide an organization's behavior. It is an important part of creating a culture of ethics within an organization, and it can help to prevent unethical behavior.

There are a number of reasons why framing ethical policies is important. First, it can help to clarify what is considered ethical behavior within an organization. This can help employees to make better decisions, and it can also help to prevent misunderstandings about what is acceptable behavior.

Second, framing ethical policies can help to create a culture of ethics within an organization. When employees know what is expected of them, they are more likely to behave ethically. This can lead to a number of benefits, such as increased trust, improved morale, and reduced risk of legal liability.

Third, framing ethical policies can help to prevent unethical behavior. When employees know that there are consequences for unethical behavior, they are less likely to engage in it. This can help to protect the organization from legal liability, financial loss, and reputational damage.

There are a number of different ways to frame ethical policies. Some organizations choose to create a code of ethics, while others choose to develop a more informal set of ethical guidelines. The best way to frame ethical policies will vary depending on the specific needs of the organization.

However, there are a few key principles that should be considered when framing ethical policies. First, the policies should be clear and concise. Employees should be able to understand what is expected of them, and they should be able to easily access the policies.

Second, the policies should be consistent with the organization's values. The policies should reflect the organization's commitment to ethics, and they should be aligned with the organization's overall mission and goals.

Third, the policies should be enforced. Employees should know that there are consequences for violating the policies, and the organization should be prepared to take action if necessary.

Framing ethical policies is an important part of creating a culture of ethics within an organization. By taking the time to frame ethical policies correctly, organizations can help to prevent unethical behavior and protect themselves from legal liability.

Here are some additional tips for framing ethical policies:

- Involve employees in the process of developing the policies. This will help to ensure that the policies are relevant and that employees are committed to them.
- Use clear and simple language. The policies should be easy to

understand and follow.

- Be specific. The policies should provide clear guidance on what is considered ethical behavior.
- Be consistent. The policies should be consistent with the organization's values and mission.
- Be enforced. The organization should be prepared to take action if the policies are violated.

By following these tips, organizations can frame ethical policies that help to create a culture of ethics and prevent unethical behavior.

1.3.3. How to Promote an Ethical Business Environment

Here are some tips on how to promote an ethical business environment in more detail:

Create a code of ethics. A code of ethics is a written document that outlines the organization's values and expectations for ethical behavior. It should be clear, concise, and easy to understand. The code of ethics should cover a wide range of ethical issues, such as conflict of interest, discrimination, privacy, and whistleblowing.

Provide training on ethics. Employees should be trained on the organization's code of ethics and how to apply it to their work. This training should be ongoing and should be tailored to the specific needs of the organization. The training should cover topics such as the importance of ethical behavior, how to identify and resolve ethical dilemmas, and the consequences of unethical behavior.

Encourage open communication. Employees should feel comfortable reporting unethical behavior without fear of retaliation. The organization should have a clear process for reporting unethical behavior and should take action promptly when allegations are made.

Employees should also be encouraged to speak up if they see something that they believe is wrong.

Set a good example. Leaders should set a good example by behaving ethically themselves. They should make it clear that ethical behavior is expected and that it will be rewarded. Leaders should also be open to feedback and should be willing to admit when they make mistakes.

Create a culture of trust and respect. Employees should feel like they are part of a team and that their contributions are valued. They should also feel like they can trust their colleagues and leaders to act ethically. The organization should create a culture where employees feel comfortable asking questions and raising concerns.

Be transparent. Employees should be kept informed about the organization's activities and decisions. This will help to build trust and make it more likely that employees will behave ethically. The organization should be transparent about its finances, its business practices, and its relationships with stakeholders.

Hold employees accountable. Employees should be held accountable for their actions. This means that there should be consequences for unethical behavior. The consequences should be fair and should be communicated to employees in advance.

Involve employees in the development of ethical policies and procedures. This will help to ensure that the policies are relevant and that employees are committed to them. Employees should be involved in the development of the code of ethics, the training program, and the process for reporting unethical behavior.

Provide employees with access to resources on ethics, such as training materials, online resources, and mentors. This will help employees to make informed decisions and to resolve ethical dilemmas. The organization should provide employees with access to resources that can help them to understand ethical issues and to make ethical decisions.

Create a culture of feedback and dialogue. This will help to identify and address ethical issues early on. The organization should create a culture where employees feel comfortable raising concerns and asking questions. The organization should also have a process for resolving ethical issues in a fair and timely manner.

Be prepared to take action when ethical violations occur. This will help to deter future violations and to protect the organization's reputation. The organization should have a process for investigating and responding to ethical violations. The process should be fair and should be communicated to employees in advance.

By following these tips, organizations can create a business environment that is ethical, productive, and sustainable.

1.4. Why Ethical Problems Occur in Business

Ethical problems in business can be broadly defined as any action or behavior that violates the ethical standards of an organization or society. These standards can vary depending on the specific organization or society, but they typically include things like honesty, integrity, fairness, and respect for others.

Ethical problems occur in business for a variety of reasons, including:

- **Pressure to meet financial goals.** In today's competitive business environment, there is often pressure to meet financial goals, even if it means cutting corners or bending the rules. This pressure can lead to unethical behavior, such as falsifying financial records or engaging in price-fixing.
- **Lack of ethical leadership.** When leaders behave

unethically, it sends a message to employees that unethical behavior is acceptable. This can create a culture of unethical behavior within an organization.

- **Lack of training on ethics.** Many employees do not receive training on ethics, which can leave them unprepared to make ethical decisions. This can lead to unethical behavior, even if employees do not intend to do anything wrong.
- **Confusing or unclear ethical standards.** If an organization's ethical standards are confusing or unclear, it can be difficult for employees to know what is expected of them. This can lead to ethical lapses.
- **Lack of consequences for unethical behavior.** When employees who engage in unethical behavior are not held accountable, it sends a message that unethical behavior is tolerated. This can embolden other employees to engage in unethical behavior.

These are just some of the reasons why ethical problems occur in business. It is important for organizations to take steps to prevent ethical problems, such as creating a code of ethics, providing training on ethics, and holding employees accountable for their actions.

Here are some additional reasons why ethical problems occur in business:

- **Conflict of interest.** This occurs when an individual has competing interests that could influence their judgment. For example, an employee who is responsible for approving contracts may have a conflict of interest if they are also a vendor to the company.
- **Discrimination.** This occurs when individuals are treated differently based on their race, gender, religion, or other

protected characteristic. For example, an employer may discriminate against a job applicant because of their race.

- **Privacy violations.** This occurs when an individual's personal information is used or disclosed without their consent. For example, an employer may violate an employee's privacy by monitoring their email without their knowledge.
- **Whistleblowing.** This occurs when an individual reports unethical or illegal activity within an organization. Whistleblowers often face retaliation from their employers, which can discourage others from reporting unethical behavior.

Ethical problems can have a significant impact on businesses, including:

- **Financial losses.** Unethical behavior can lead to financial losses, such as fines, lawsuits, and damage to the company's reputation.
- **Damage to reputation.** When an organization is involved in an ethical scandal, its reputation can be damaged. This can make it difficult for the organization to attract customers, investors, and employees.
- **Loss of trust.** When employees see that their leaders are behaving unethically, they may lose trust in the organization. This can lead to decreased productivity and increased turnover.
- **Legal liability.** Organizations that engage in unethical behavior may be subject to legal liability. This could include fines, lawsuits, and even criminal charges.

It is important for businesses to take steps to prevent ethical problems. By creating a culture of ethics and holding employees accountable for their actions, businesses can reduce the risk of ethical problems and protect their reputations.

1.5. Workplace Ethics And Laws

Workplace ethics and laws are both important concepts that guide behavior in the workplace. However, there are some key differences between the two.

- **Ethics are based on moral principles, while laws are based on codified rules.** Ethics are based on what is considered right and wrong, while laws are based on what is legally permissible. This means that ethics can be more subjective than laws, as there is no single set of ethical principles that everyone agrees on. Laws, on the other hand, are more objective, as they are based on rules that have been created by governments or other authority figures.
- **Ethics are aspirational, while laws are mandatory.** Ethics are aspirational in the sense that they outline what we should strive to do, while laws are mandatory in the sense that they outline what we must do. This means that ethics are not always enforceable, while laws are always enforceable. For example, an organization may have an ethical code that prohibits discrimination, but this code would not be enforceable by law unless discrimination was also illegal.
- **Ethics are more focused on the individual, while laws are more focused on the organization.** Ethics are more focused on the individual in the sense that they outline how individuals should behave. Laws, on the other hand, are more focused on the organization in the sense that they outline how organizations should behave. For example, an organization may have an ethical code that prohibits

employees from accepting bribes, but this code would not be enforceable by law unless bribery was also illegal.

- **Learn about the ethical code of your organization.** Most organizations have an ethical code that outlines the organization's ethical standards. This code can be a valuable resource for understanding what is expected of you in the workplace.
- **Be aware of the laws that govern your workplace.** The laws that govern your workplace will vary depending on your location and the industry you work in. However, there are some general laws that apply to all workplaces, such as anti-discrimination laws and labor laws.
- **Talk to your manager or HR department if you have any questions about workplace ethics or laws.** Your manager or HR department can provide guidance on how to apply the ethical code and the laws to your specific situation.

1.6. An Ethical Code of Conduct in Global Business

An ethical code of conduct in global business is a set of principles that guide the behavior of businesses and their employees when conducting business internationally. These principles are typically based on a set of universal values, such as honesty, integrity, and respect for others.

Ethical codes of conduct are important for a number of reasons. First, they can help to ensure that businesses behave in a responsible and ethical manner, even when they are operating in different countries with different cultures and legal systems. Second, they can help to protect businesses from legal liability, as they can demonstrate that the business has taken steps to prevent unethical behavior. Third, they can help to build trust with customers, partners, and other stakeholders.

There are a number of different ethical codes of conduct that are used in global business. Some of the most well-known codes include the UN Global Compact, the OECD Guidelines for Multinational Enterprises, and the Caux Principles. These codes are all based on the same set of universal values, but they may differ in their specific emphasis and application.

The UN Global Compact is a set of ten principles that cover human rights, labor, the environment, and anti-corruption. The OECD Guidelines for Multinational Enterprises are a set of voluntary principles that cover a wide range of business practices, including employment and industrial relations, environment, information disclosure, and combating bribery. The Caux Principles are a set of six principles that focus on the responsibilities of businesses to stakeholders, including customers, employees, shareholders, suppliers, and communities.

In addition to these well-known codes, there are also a number of other ethical codes of conduct that are used in global business. These codes may be developed by individual businesses, industry associations, or other organizations.

The use of ethical codes of conduct in global business is growing. This is due to a number of factors, including the increasing globalization of business, the growing awareness of the importance of ethics, and the increasing pressure from stakeholders for businesses to behave in an ethical manner.

Here are some of the benefits of using an ethical code of conduct in global business:

- **Increased trust:** An ethical code of conduct can help to build trust with customers, partners, and other stakeholders. This is because it demonstrates that the business is committed to behaving in a responsible and ethical manner.

- **Reduced risk:** An ethical code of conduct can help to reduce the risk of legal liability. This is because it can demonstrate that the business has taken steps to prevent unethical behavior.

- **Improved decision-making:** An ethical code of conduct can help businesses to make better decisions. This is because it provides a framework for businesses to consider the ethical implications of their decisions.

- **Enhanced reputation:** An ethical code of conduct can enhance the reputation of a business. This is because it demonstrates that the business is committed to behaving in a responsible and ethical manner.

Overall, an ethical code of conduct can be a valuable tool for businesses that operate in the global marketplace. It can help businesses to build trust, reduce risk, improve decision-making, and enhance their reputation.

1.7. Government Protection Policies Against Illegal Business Practices

Government protection policies against illegal business practices are laws and regulations that are designed to protect consumers, employees, and the environment from unethical and harmful business practices. These policies can vary from country to country, but they typically cover a wide range of areas, including:

- **Antitrust:** Antitrust laws are designed to prevent businesses from engaging in anti-competitive practices, such as price-fixing and collusion.

- **Consumer protection:** Consumer protection laws are

designed to protect consumers from unfair and deceptive business practices, such as false advertising and misleading labeling.

- **Labor law:** Labor laws are designed to protect employees from exploitation, such as wage theft and discrimination.
- **Environmental protection:** Environmental protection laws are designed to protect the environment from pollution and other harmful activities.

Government protection policies against illegal business practices are important for a number of reasons. First, they can help to ensure that businesses compete fairly and that consumers are not taken advantage of. Second, they can help to protect employees from exploitation and ensure that they are treated fairly. Third, they can help to protect the environment and ensure that businesses do not pollute or damage the environment.

There are a number of different ways that government protection policies against illegal business practices can be enforced. In some cases, businesses may be required to obtain a license or permit before they can operate. In other cases, businesses may be subject to inspections or audits. And in some cases, businesses may be fined or even shut down if they violate the law.

The effectiveness of government protection policies against illegal business practices varies from country to country. In some countries, these policies are well-enforced and businesses are held accountable for their actions. In other countries, these policies are not as well-enforced and businesses may get away with breaking the law.

However, even in countries where these policies are not as well-enforced, they can still play an important role in deterring illegal business practices and protecting consumers, employees, and the environment.

1.8. Influence of Interest Groups on the Government

Interest groups are organizations that seek to influence public policy on behalf of a particular group of people or organizations. They can be very influential in the political process, and they can have a significant impact on the outcome of elections and the passage of legislation.

There are many different types of interest groups, including business groups, labor unions, environmental groups, and social welfare groups. These groups can influence the government in a number of ways, including:

- **Lobbying:** Lobbying is the process of trying to influence government officials to support a particular policy or position. Interest groups can lobby government officials directly, or they can work through other channels, such as the media or the public.
- **Contributing to political campaigns:** Interest groups can contribute money to political campaigns, which can help to elect candidates who are sympathetic to their interests.
- **Grassroots organizing:** Interest groups can organize their members and supporters to contact their elected officials and express their views on particular issues.
- **Public relations:** Interest groups can use public relations to generate positive publicity for their cause and to try to sway public opinion.

The influence of interest groups on the government varies from country to country. In some countries, interest groups have a very strong influence, while in other countries, they have less influence. The level of influence that interest groups have also varies depending on the issue. For example, interest groups may have more influence on issues that are closely related to their particular interests.

The influence of interest groups on the government can be a controversial issue. Some people believe that interest groups have too much influence and that they can unduly influence the political process. Others believe that interest groups are a necessary part of the political process and that they can help to ensure that the views of different groups are represented.

Ultimately, the influence of interest groups on the government is a complex issue that depends on a number of factors, including the political system, the culture, and the specific issue at stake.

Chapter 2. Corporation and Stakeholder Ethics

2.1. Impact of Business Decisions on Stakeholders

2.2. Ethics of Emplyoyer- Employee Realtionship and its Effects on Stakeholders

2.3. Organization of Modern Corporation and Interaction with Stakeholders

2.4. Whistle-Blower Act and Employee Rights: Privacy and Safety

2.4.1 Salient Features of Whistle-Blower Act

2.4.2. Employee Rights: Privacy at Work Place

2.5. Employee Rights : Safety at Workplace

2.6. Collective Bargaining and Role of Management in Implementing Ethics

Introduction:

Corporation and stakeholder ethics is a branch of business ethics that deals with the moral obligations of corporations to their stakeholders. Stakeholders are individuals or groups that have a stake in the corporation, such as shareholders, employees, customers, suppliers, and the local community.

The basic idea of stakeholder ethics is that corporations have a responsibility to act in a way that is beneficial to all of their stakeholders, not just their shareholders. This means that corporations should not only focus on making a profit, but they should also consider the interests of all of their stakeholders when making decisions.

There are a number of different ethical theories that can be used to guide corporate decision-making. Some of the most common ethical theories include:

- Utilitarianism: This theory argues that the best action is the one that produces the greatest good for the greatest number of people.
- Deontology: This theory argues that actions are right or wrong regardless of their consequences.
- Virtue ethics: This theory argues that the right action is the one that is consistent with the virtues of courage, honesty, and compassion.

Corporations can use these ethical theories to help them make decisions that are beneficial to all of their stakeholders. For example, a corporation might use utilitarianism to decide whether to build a new factory that would create jobs and boost the local economy, even if it would also pollute the environment. The corporation would need to weigh the benefits of the new factory to the stakeholders, such as the employees, the local community, and the environment, to determine whether it is the right decision.

Stakeholder ethics is an important concept because it helps corporations to balance the interests of different stakeholders. This can lead to better decision-making and a more sustainable business model. It can also help to build trust and goodwill with stakeholders, which can be beneficial to the corporation in the long run.

2.1. Impact of Business Decisions on Stakeholders

The impact of business decisions on stakeholders can be far-reaching and long-lasting. Some of the most common impacts include:

- **Financial impact:** Business decisions can have a significant impact on the financial well-being of stakeholders. For example, a decision to lay off employees can have a negative impact on the financial security of those employees and their families. A decision to outsource production to a lower-cost country can have a negative impact on the jobs and wages of workers in the home country.

- **Social impact:** Business decisions can also have a significant impact on the social well-being of stakeholders. For example, a decision to open a new factory in a developing country can have a positive impact on the local economy by creating jobs and stimulating economic growth. However, it can also have a negative impact on the environment and the health of local residents if the factory is not operated in a sustainable manner.

- **Environmental impact:** Business decisions can also have a significant impact on the environment. For example, a decision to use a more polluting fuel source can have a negative impact on air quality and contribute to climate change. A decision to dump hazardous waste into a river can have a negative impact on the health of fish and other wildlife.

- **Reputational impact:** Business decisions can also have a significant impact on the reputation of stakeholders. For example, a decision to engage in unethical behavior, such as price-fixing or environmental pollution, can damage the reputation of a company and its executives. This can lead to lost customers, investors, and employees.

It is important for businesses to carefully consider the potential impact of their decisions on all stakeholders before making a decision. By taking into account the interests of all stakeholders, businesses can make decisions that are more likely to be beneficial to the long-term success of the business and the well-being of society.

Here are some examples of how business decisions can have a positive or negative impact on stakeholders:

- **Positive impact:**
  - A decision to invest in research and development can lead to new products and services that benefit customers and the environment.
  - A decision to adopt sustainable business practices can reduce the environmental impact of a business and improve the quality of life for local communities.
  - A decision to give back to the community through charitable donations or volunteer programs can build goodwill and support for a business.
- **Negative impact:**
  - A decision to outsource production to a lower-cost country can lead to job losses in the home country.
  - A decision to pollute the environment can damage the health of local residents and wildlife.
  - A decision to engage in unethical behavior, such as price-fixing or bribery, can damage the reputation of a business and its executives.

By understanding the potential impact of their decisions on stakeholders, businesses can make more informed decisions that are more likely to be beneficial to all

2.2. Ethics of Emplyoyer- Employee Realtionship and its Effects on Stakeholders

The ethics of employer-employee relationship refers to the moral obligations that employers and employees have to each other. These obligations are based on the principle of fairness and respect.

Employers have a number of ethical obligations to their employees, including:

- **Providing a safe and healthy workplace.** Employers have a legal and ethical obligation to provide a safe and healthy workplace for their employees. This means taking steps to prevent accidents and injuries, and to protect employees from exposure to hazardous materials.
- **Paying employees fairly.** Employers have a moral obligation to pay their employees fairly for their work. This means paying them a living wage, and ensuring that they are compensated for overtime and other work-related expenses.
- **Treating employees with respect.** Employers have a moral obligation to treat their employees with respect. This means listening to their concerns, giving them fair opportunities for advancement, and avoiding discrimination and harassment.

Employees also have a number of ethical obligations to their employers, including:

- **Performing their duties to the best of their ability.** Employees have a moral obligation to perform their duties to the best of their ability. This means being honest and hardworking, and meeting deadlines and expectations.
- **Being respectful of their employer's property and resources.** Employees have a moral obligation to be respectful of their employer's property and resources. This means using them wisely and avoiding waste.

- **Keeping confidential information confidential.** Employees have a moral obligation to keep confidential information confidential. This means not sharing it with unauthorized people or using it for personal gain.

When employers and employees treat each other fairly and with respect, it creates a positive work environment that is beneficial to everyone involved. Employees are more likely to be productive and engaged, and they are less likely to leave the company. This can lead to increased profits for the employer, and it can also benefit customers and the community.

However, when employers and employees treat each other unethically, it can have a negative impact on stakeholders. Employees may be less productive and engaged, and they may be more likely to leave the company. This can lead to decreased profits for the employer, and it can also harm customers and the community.

Here are some specific examples of ethical issues that can arise in the employer-employee relationship:

- **Discrimination and harassment.** Employers have a legal and ethical obligation to create a workplace free from discrimination and harassment. This means not discriminating against employees on the basis of race, color, religion, sex, national origin, age, disability, or other protected categories. It also means not tolerating harassment of employees, regardless of the source.
- **Wage theft.** Employers have a legal and ethical obligation to pay their employees fairly. This means paying them the wages they are owed, including overtime pay and any other legally required compensation. Wage theft is a serious problem that can have a devastating impact on employees.

- **Privacy violations.** Employers have a legal and ethical obligation to respect the privacy of their employees. This means not collecting or using personal information about employees without their consent. It also means not disclosing confidential information about employees to unauthorized people.
- **Safety violations.** Employers have a legal and ethical obligation to provide a safe workplace for their employees. This means taking steps to prevent accidents and injuries, and to protect employees from exposure to hazardous materials. Safety violations can lead to serious injuries or even death.

By understanding the ethics of employer-employee relationship, employers and employees can create a positive and productive work environment that is beneficial to everyone involved.

2.3 Organization of Modern Corporation and Interaction with Stakeholders

The organization of modern corporations has evolved over time to reflect the changing needs of businesses and the demands of stakeholders. In the early days of corporate America, corporations were largely hierarchical organizations with a clear separation between management and labor. However, this model has become increasingly outdated as businesses have become more complex and globalized.

Modern corporations are now more likely to be organized around a network of teams and individuals who work together to achieve common goals. This more fluid and collaborative approach to organization is better suited to the challenges of the 21st century economy.

One of the most important changes in the organization of modern corporations is the increased emphasis on stakeholder engagement. Stakeholders are individuals or groups who have a vested interest in the success of a corporation, such as employees, customers, suppliers, investors, and the local community. In the past, corporations often treated stakeholders as little more than nuisances. However, modern corporations understand that they need to build relationships with stakeholders in order to be successful.

There are a number of ways that corporations can interact with stakeholders. One way is to establish formal channels of communication, such as stakeholder advisory boards or social media forums. Corporations can also use informal channels of communication, such as employee surveys or customer focus groups. By listening to the concerns of stakeholders and responding to their feedback, corporations can build trust and goodwill.

The organization of modern corporations and its interaction with stakeholders is a complex and ever-evolving process. However, by understanding the needs of stakeholders and building relationships with them, corporations can create a more sustainable and successful business model.

2.4. Whistle-Blower Act and Employee Rights: Privacy and Safety

The Whistleblowers Protection Act, 2011 (WPA) is an Act of the Parliament of India that provides a mechanism to investigate alleged corruption and misuse of power by public servants and also protect anyone who exposes alleged wrongdoing in government bodies, projects and offices. The wrongdoing might be in the form of fraud, corruption or mismanagement. The Act will also ensure punishment for false or frivolous complaints.

The WPA was passed by the Lok Sabha on 27 December 2011 and by the Rajya Sabha on 21 February 2014. It received the President's assent on 9 May 2014.

The WPA was preceded by the Public Interest Disclosure and Protection of Persons Making the Disclosures Bill, 2010. The Bill was introduced in the Lok Sabha in August 2010. It was referred to the Department Related Parliamentary Standing Committee on Personnel, Public Grievances, Law and Justice. The Committee made a number of recommendations, which were incorporated in the WPA.

The WPA is based on the principle that it is in the public interest to encourage people to report suspected wrongdoing by public servants. The Act provides a number of safeguards to protect whistleblowers from retaliation. Whistleblowers are protected from dismissal, demotion, transfer, or other adverse action. They are also protected from harassment or intimidation.

The WPA also provides for a number of remedies for whistleblowers who are retaliated against. Whistleblowers can file a complaint with the Central Vigilance Commission (CVC). The CVC is an independent body that is responsible for investigating and resolving whistleblower complaints. If the CVC finds that a whistleblower has been retaliated against, it can order the employer to take corrective action, such as reinstating the whistleblower or awarding them back pay. The CVC can also file a lawsuit against the employer on behalf of the whistleblower.

The WPA is an important law that protects whistleblowers from retaliation. The WPA helps to ensure that whistleblowers can report wrongdoing without fear of reprisal, and that those who violate the law are held accountable.

2.4.1. The Salient Features Of The Whistleblowers Protection Act, 2011 (WPA)

- **Protection of whistleblowers:** The WPA protects whistleblowers from retaliation. This includes protection from dismissal, demotion, transfer, or other adverse action. Whistleblowers are also protected from harassment or intimidation.

- **Remedies for whistleblowers:** Whistleblowers who are retaliated against have a number of remedies available to them. They can file a complaint with the Central Vigilance Commission (CVC), which is an independent body that is responsible for investigating and resolving whistleblower complaints. If the CVC finds that a whistleblower has been retaliated against, it can order the employer to take corrective action, such as reinstating the whistleblower or awarding them back pay. The CVC can also file a lawsuit against the employer on behalf of the whistleblower.

- **Punishment for false or frivolous complaints:** The WPA also provides for punishment for false or frivolous complaints. Anyone who makes a false or frivolous complaint under the WPA can be punished with imprisonment for up to two years, or a fine of up to 30,000 rupees, or both.

- **Establishment of Central Whistleblower Protection Cell:** The WPA establishes a Central Whistleblower Protection Cell (CWPC) within the CVC. The CWPC is responsible for receiving and processing complaints from whistleblowers. It is also responsible for investigating complaints and taking appropriate action.

- **Establishment of State Whistleblower Protection Cells:** The WPA also allows states to establish their own Whistleblower Protection Cells. State Whistleblower Protection Cells will have the same powers and functions as the CWPC.

- **Confidentiality of identity:** The WPA protects the confidentiality of the identity of whistleblowers. The identity of a whistleblower will not be disclosed without their consent, except in certain circumstances, such as when it is necessary to investigate the complaint or to protect the public interest.
- **Time limits for investigation:** The WPA sets time limits for the investigation of whistleblower complaints. The CVC or the State Whistleblower Protection Cell must complete the investigation of a complaint within 90 days of its receipt.
- **Appeals:** Whistleblowers who are dissatisfied with the decision of the CVC or the State Whistleblower Protection Cell can appeal to the Central Administrative Tribunal (CAT). The CAT is an independent body that is responsible for hearing appeals against the decisions of government agencies.

The WPA is an important law that protects whistleblowers from retaliation and provides them with a number of remedies if they are retaliated against. The WPA helps to ensure that whistleblowers can report wrongdoing without fear of reprisal, and that those who violate the law are held accountable.

2.4.2. Employees Right: Privacy At The Workplace

Privacy at the workplace refers to the right of employees to have their personal information protected from unauthorized access, collection, use, or disclosure by their employers. This includes information such as their email, phone calls, internet browsing history, and social media activity.

There are a number of laws that protect employee privacy in the workplace, including the following:

- **The Indian Constitution:** The Indian Constitution guarantees the right to privacy to all citizens. This right is protected by Article 21 of the Constitution, which states that no person shall be deprived of their life or personal liberty except according to procedure established by law.

Internet Usage and Email: In general, employees have no expectation of privacy when using the internet or email at work. Employers have the right to monitor and review employee activity, including emails and internet browsing history, if there is a "legitimate business purpose" for doing so. This can include things like preventing fraud, protecting trade secrets, or ensuring that employees are not using work time for personal activities. There are a few exceptions to this rule. For example, employees may have a reasonable expectation of privacy in their personal emails if they are sent using a personal email account and not the company's email system. Additionally, some states have laws that provide additional privacy protections for employees.

Phone calls and Voicemail Messages: In general, employees have no expectation of privacy when using company phones or voice mail systems. Employers have the right to monitor and review employee phone calls and voice mails if there is a "legitimate business purpose" for doing so. This can include things like preventing fraud, protecting trade secrets, or ensuring that employees are not using work time for personal activities.

There are a few exceptions to this rule. For example, employees may have a reasonable expectation of privacy in their personal phone calls if they are made using a personal cell phone and not the company's phone system. Additionally, some states have laws that provide additional privacy protections for employees.

Post Hiring Drug Testing: The privacy of employees who are subjected to post-hiring drug testing in the workplace is a complex issue that depends on a number of factors, including the laws of the state in which the company is located, the company's drug testing policy, and the employee's job duties.

In general, employers have the right to conduct post-hiring drug testing if they have a "legitimate business reason" for doing so. This can include things like ensuring the safety of employees and customers, preventing accidents, and complying with federal or state laws. However, employers are not allowed to discriminate against employees based on the results of a drug test.

The laws of the state in which the company is located may also impact the privacy of employees who are subjected to post-hiring drug testing. For example, some states require employers to obtain a warrant before conducting a drug test, and some states prohibit employers from testing employees for certain types of drugs.

Video Surveillance: Video surveillance privacy at work is a complex issue that depends on a number of factors, including the laws of the state in which the company is located, the company's video surveillance policy, and the employee's job duties.

In general, employers have the right to install video surveillance in the workplace if they have a "legitimate business reason" for doing so. This can include things like preventing theft, ensuring the safety of employees and customers, and deterring crime. However, employers are not allowed to use video surveillance to spy on employees or to violate their privacy.

The laws of the state in which the company is located may also impact the privacy of employees who are subjected to video surveillance. For example, some states require employers to obtain a warrant before installing video surveillance, and some states prohibit employers from installing video surveillance in certain areas, such as bathrooms and locker rooms.

The company's video surveillance policy will also play a role in determining the privacy of employees who are subjected to video surveillance. This policy should be clear and concise, and it should be distributed to all employees. The policy should also state the reasons for the video surveillance, the areas that are being monitored, and the procedures for accessing and reviewing the video footage.

Finally, the employee's job duties may also impact the privacy of their video surveillance. For example, employees who are in safety-sensitive positions may be subject to more extensive video surveillance than employees who are not in safety-sensitive positions.

If you have concerns about the privacy of your video surveillance, you should talk to your supervisor or human resources department. They should be able to answer any questions you have about the company's video surveillance policy and the laws of the state in which you work.

2.5 Employees Right: Safety At The Workplace

Workplace safety is the prevention of injuries and illnesses in the workplace. It is important for employers and employees to work together to create a safe workplace.Detailed explanation of employees' rights to safety at the workplace:

- **The Right to a Safe Workplace:** Employees have the right to a safe workplace free from recognized hazards that are likely to cause death or serious physical harm. This right is protected by a number of federal and state laws, including the Occupational Safety and Health Act (OSHA). OSHA sets and enforces standards for workplace safety, and it investigates complaints of workplace hazards.
- **The Right to Know About Workplace Hazards:** Employees have the right to know about the hazards in their workplace and the steps that they can take to protect themselves from

harm. Employers are required to provide employees with information about the hazards in their workplace, including the risks associated with those hazards, the steps that employees can take to protect themselves, and the procedures for reporting workplace hazards.

- **The Right to Participate in Safety and Health Matters:** Employees have the right to participate in safety and health matters in their workplace. This includes the right to be informed about workplace hazards, the right to participate in safety and health training, and the right to file complaints about workplace hazards.

- **The Right to Refuse Unsafe Work:** Employees have the right to refuse to work in a situation that they believe is unsafe. This right is known as the "right to refuse unsafe work." Employees can refuse to work if they believe that the work is likely to cause them serious injury or death. However, employees must first try to resolve the safety issue with their employer. If the employer cannot resolve the safety issue, then the employee can refuse to work.

- **The Right to Protection from Retaliation:** Employees have the right to be protected from retaliation for exercising their workplace safety rights. This means that employees cannot be fired, demoted, or otherwise penalized for reporting a workplace hazard, participating in safety and health training, or refusing to work in an unsafe situation.

These are just some of the most important employee rights related to safety in the workplace. Employees who believe that their safety rights have been violated should contact their employer, OSHA, or a lawyer

Here are some specific requirements of the Factories Act related to safety at the workplace:

- **Employers must provide a safe workplace.** This includes providing adequate lighting, ventilation, and sanitation facilities. Employers must also ensure that machinery is properly maintained and that there are no exposed wires or other hazards.
- **Employers must provide personal protective equipment (PPE).** This includes things like hard hats, safety glasses, and gloves. Employers must ensure that employees wear PPE when it is necessary to protect them from hazards.
- **Employers must train employees on safety procedures.** This training should cover the specific hazards in the workplace and the steps that employees can take to protect themselves.
- **Employers must investigate accidents.** If an accident occurs in the workplace, the employer must investigate the accident to determine the cause and to take corrective action.
- **Employers must take corrective action.** If an accident occurs in the workplace, the employer must take corrective action to prevent the accident from happening again. This may include repairing machinery, providing additional training, or changing work procedures.

2.6. Collective Bargaining and Role of Managemenent in Impelmenting Ethics

Collective bargaining is a process in which representatives of a union negotiate with an employer on behalf of a group of employees. The goal of collective bargaining is to reach an agreement on wages, benefits, working conditions, and other terms of employment.

Collective bargaining is an important tool for workers because it allows them to have a say in their working conditions. Without collective bargaining, workers would be at the mercy of their employers, who could set wages and conditions without any input from the workers.

Collective bargaining is also important for employers because it can help to create a more stable and productive workforce. When workers are happy with their wages and conditions, they are more likely to be productive and less likely to go on strike.

The role of management in implementing ethics in the workplace is to create a culture of ethics and to ensure that all employees are aware of the company's ethical standards. Management can do this by:

- **Communicating the company's ethical standards to all employees.** This can be done through training, employee handbooks, and other communication channels.
- **Providing employees with the resources they need to make ethical decisions.** This includes training on ethics, access to ethical decision-making tools, and support from management.
- **Encouraging employees to report unethical behavior.** Employees should feel comfortable reporting unethical behavior without fear of retaliation.
- **Investigating and addressing all reports of unethical behavior.** Management should take all reports of unethical behavior seriously and investigate them promptly.
- **Disciplining employees who engage in unethical behavior.** Employees who engage in unethical behavior should be disciplined appropriately.

Collective bargaining can play a role in implementing ethics in the workplace by providing a forum for employees to raise concerns about ethical issues. The union can also negotiate for ethical standards to be included in the collective bargaining agreement.

The collective bargaining process typically involves the following steps:

1. The union selects a bargaining team to represent the workers.
2. The bargaining team meets with the employer to discuss the terms of employment.
3. The two sides negotiate until they reach an agreement or until they reach an impasse.
4. If the two sides reach an agreement, the agreement is put in writing and signed by both parties.
5. If the two sides reach an impasse, the union may call a strike or the employer may lock out the workers.

Collective bargaining can be a complex and challenging process, but it is an important tool for workers and employers alike. By working together, workers and employers can reach an agreement that is fair to both sides and that benefits the entire workforce.

Here are some of the advantages of collective bargaining:

- **Increased wages and benefits:** Collective bargaining can lead to increased wages and benefits for workers. This is because unions have more power to negotiate with employers than individual workers do.
- **Improved working conditions:** Collective bargaining can also lead to improved working conditions for workers. This includes things like shorter hours, safer workplaces, and more vacation time.
- **Job security:** Collective bargaining can help to protect jobs. This is because unions can negotiate for clauses in collective bargaining agreements that make it more difficult for employers to lay off workers.
- **A voice in the workplace:** Collective bargaining gives

workers a voice in the workplace. This means that workers have a say in things like their wages, benefits, and working conditions.

Here are some of the disadvantages of collective bargaining:

- **Strikes:** Collective bargaining can lead to strikes. This is when workers refuse to work until their demands are met. Strikes can be disruptive to businesses and can hurt the economy.
- **Costs:** Collective bargaining can be expensive for both employers and unions. This is because it requires time and resources to negotiate a collective bargaining agreement.
- **Complexity:** Collective bargaining can be a complex process. This is because there are a lot of factors to consider, such as wages, benefits, working conditions, and job security.
- **Impasses:** Sometimes, collective bargaining can reach an impasse. This means that the two sides cannot agree on a contract. This can lead to strikes or lockouts.

Overall, collective bargaining is a complex process with both advantages and disadvantages. However, it is an important tool for workers to have a say in their working conditions.

The Marketing Concept And The Agreement As A Contract:

The marketing concept views collective bargaining as a contract for the sale of labor. This is a market-based approach that justifies collective bargaining on the grounds that it gives workers a voice in the sale of their labor. The same objective rules that apply to commercial contracts are also applied to union-management relationships, since they are considered to be commercial in nature.

- **According to this theory,** employees sell their labor only on terms that have been collectively determined through the process of collective bargaining. This is necessary due to the uncertainty of trade cycles, the spirit of mass production, and competition for jobs. Trade unions provide strength to individual workers by enabling them to resist the pressure of circumstances and to face an unbalanced and disadvantageous situation created by employers. The goal of trade union policy is to give each individual worker a share of the indispensability of labor as a whole.

- **It is difficult to say** whether workers have achieved bargaining equality with employers. However, collective bargaining has created a new relationship in which it is difficult for employers to dispense with workers without facing the relatively greater collective strength of the workforce.

The Governmental Concept And The Agreement As A Law:

The **governmental concept** of collective bargaining views it as a system of government in the workplace. This is a political approach that sees the union and management as sharing power over the workers. The union, as the representative of the workers, uses its power to negotiate agreements that are in the best interests of its members. The agreement is then viewed as a law that is binding on both parties.

The agreement is not simply a contract between two parties, but rather a constitution that establishes the rules of the workplace. It sets out the procedures for making, enforcing, and interpreting these rules. The agreement also limits the power of both parties, and provides a mechanism for resolving disputes. This creates a system of joint industrial government, in which the union and management share power and responsibility for the workforce

The Managerial Concept/ Industrial Relation Concept As Jointly Decided Directives:

The **managerial concept** of collective bargaining views it as a system of industrial governance. This is a functional approach that sees the union and management as partners in running the business. The union representative is involved in the managerial role, and discussions take place in good faith to reach agreements that are in the best interests of both parties.

The union and management work together to make decisions on matters that are important to both of them. This creates a system of joint governance, in which the union and management share power and responsibility for the workplace.

The managerial concept of collective bargaining is a more recent development than the marketing concept or the governmental concept. It is based on the idea that the union and management have a shared interest in the success of the business, and that they can work together to achieve that success.

The Industrial Disputes Act of 1947 in India established a legal basis for union participation in management. This act recognized the right of unions to be represented on company committees and to have a say in decision-making. The act also provided for arbitration of disputes between unions and management.

The managerial concept of collective bargaining is still evolving. However, it is becoming increasingly accepted as a way to manage industrial relations in a way that is fair to both workers and employers.

Chapter 3. Business, Governanace and Societal Ethics

3.1 Role and Responsibilities of the Organization towards Government and Society in Business Ethics

The role and responsibilities of an organization towards government and society in business ethics are complex and ever-evolving. However, there are some key principles that can guide organizations in their approach to these relationships.

One of the most important responsibilities of an organization is to obey the law. This includes complying with all applicable laws and regulations, both domestic and international. Organizations should also avoid engaging in any unethical or illegal practices, such as bribery or corruption.

In addition to legal compliance, organizations also have a responsibility to act in a socially responsible manner. This means taking into account the impact of their activities on the environment, on society, and on the communities in which they operate. Organizations should strive to minimize their negative impact and to maximize their positive impact.

Organizations should also be good corporate citizens. This means being involved in the community and giving back to the society that has helped them to succeed. Organizations can do this by supporting local charities, by providing scholarships, or by volunteering their time and resources.

Finally, organizations should be transparent in their dealings with government and society. This means being open and honest about their activities, and being accountable for their decisions. Organizations should also be willing to listen to feedback and to make changes when necessary.

By following these principles, organizations can play a positive role in society and build a strong reputation for business ethics.

Here are some specific examples of how organizations can fulfill their responsibilities towards government and society in business ethics:

- **Paying taxes:** Organizations should pay all taxes and duties that are legally due. This helps to fund government services and programs that benefit society as a whole.

- **Providing safe working conditions:** Organizations should provide safe and healthy working conditions for their employees. This is not only the right thing to do, but it is also good for business. A safe and healthy workforce is more productive and less likely to be absent from work.
- **Protecting the environment:** Organizations should take steps to protect the environment. This includes reducing pollution, conserving resources, and using sustainable practices.
- **Giving back to the community:** Organizations should support local charities and community organizations. This can help to improve the quality of life for people in the communities where they operate.
- **Being transparent:** Organizations should be open and honest about their activities. This includes disclosing financial information, reporting on environmental impacts, and providing information about their corporate governance practices.
- **Being accountable:** Organizations should be accountable for their decisions and actions. This means being willing to listen to feedback and to make changes when necessary.

By fulfilling their responsibilities towards government and society, organizations can build a strong reputation for business ethics and make a positive contribution to the world.

3.2 Types of Responsibilities

1. The Economics Responsibilities:

The economics responsibilities of a business refer to the duties that a business has to society and to the economy. These responsibilities are important because they help to ensure that businesses operate in a way that is beneficial to everyone.

Here are some of the key economics responsibilities of a business:

- **Creating jobs:** Businesses create jobs by investing in new businesses and expanding existing ones. This helps to boost the economy and improve the standard of living for people in the community.
- **Providing goods and services:** Businesses provide goods and services that people need and want. This helps to meet the demand for goods and services and to improve the quality of life for people.
- **Investing in research and development:** Businesses invest in research and development to develop new products and services. This helps to drive innovation and economic growth.

2. Legal responsibilities:

Legal responsibilities refer to the duties that an organization has to obey the law. These responsibilities are important because they help to ensure that organizations operate in a way that is fair and just.

Here are some of the key legal responsibilities of an organization:

- **Obeying the law:** Organizations have a responsibility to obey all applicable laws and regulations, both domestic and international. This includes laws on environmental protection, labor practices, and product safety.
- **Acting in a fair and just manner:** Organizations should act in a fair and just manner towards their employees, customers, and suppliers. This includes avoiding discrimination and

harassment, and providing a safe and healthy workplace.

- **Protecting the environment:** Organizations should take steps to protect the environment. This includes reducing pollution, conserving resources, and using sustainable practices.
- **Being transparent:** Organizations should be transparent about their activities. This includes disclosing financial information, reporting on environmental impacts, and providing information about their corporate governance practices.
- **Being accountable:** Organizations should be accountable for their decisions and actions. This means being willing to listen to feedback and to make changes when necessary.

3. Ethical Responsibilities

Ethical responsibilities refer to the duties that an organization has to act in a moral and responsible manner. These responsibilities are important because they help to ensure that organizations operate in a way that is beneficial to society as a whole.

Here are some of the key ethical responsibilities of an organization:

- **Acting with integrity:** Organizations should act with integrity and honesty in all their dealings. This includes being truthful in advertising and marketing, and avoiding deceptive or misleading practices.
- **Treating employees fairly:** Organizations should treat their employees fairly and with respect. This includes providing a safe and healthy workplace, paying fair wages, and offering opportunities for advancement.
- **Being socially responsible:** Organizations should be socially

responsible by taking into account the impact of their activities on the environment, on society, and on the communities in which they operate. This includes things like paying fair wages, providing safe working conditions, and giving back to the community.

4. Philanthropic Responsibilities

Philanthropic responsibilities refer to the duties that a business has to give back to society. These responsibilities are important because they help to make a positive impact on the world around us.

Here are some of the key philanthropic responsibilities of a business:

- **Donating to charity:** Businesses can donate money or goods to charities that support causes that they care about.
- **Volunteering:** Businesses can encourage their employees to volunteer their time to help others in the community.
- **Sponsoring events:** Businesses can sponsor events that benefit the community, such as fundraising galas or sporting events.
- **Creating social impact programs:** Businesses can create programs that address social issues, such as poverty, education, or healthcare.
- **Adopting a community:** Businesses can adopt a community and commit to supporting its needs, such as providing scholarships or funding community improvement projects.

5. Social Responsibility:

Social responsibility refers to the duties that a business has to its employees, customers, and the community in which it operates. These responsibilities are important because they help to create a more just and equitable society.

Here are some of the key social responsibilities of a business in detail:

- **Treating employees fairly:** Businesses should treat their employees fairly and with respect. This includes paying fair wages, providing a safe and healthy workplace, and offering opportunities for advancement.
  - **Paying fair wages:** Businesses should pay their employees a fair wage that is commensurate with their skills and experience. This helps to ensure that employees can meet their basic needs and have a decent standard of living.
  - **Providing a safe and healthy workplace:** Businesses should provide a safe and healthy workplace for their employees. This includes ensuring that the work environment is free from hazards and that employees have access to health and safety training.
  - **Offering opportunities for advancement:** Businesses should offer opportunities for advancement to their employees. This helps to motivate employees and give them a sense of purpose.
- **Providing quality products and services:** Businesses should provide quality products and services that meet the needs of their customers. This includes being truthful in advertising and marketing, and avoiding deceptive or misleading practices.
  - **Being truthful in advertising and marketing:** Businesses should be truthful in their advertising and marketing materials. This means not making false or misleading claims about their products or services.
  - **Avoiding deceptive or misleading practices:** Businesses should avoid deceptive or misleading practices, such as bait-

and-switch tactics or false advertising.

- **Being environmentally friendly:** Businesses should take steps to protect the environment. This includes reducing pollution, conserving resources, and using sustainable practices.

    ○ **Reducing pollution:** Businesses should reduce their environmental impact by minimizing the amount of pollution they produce. This can be done by using cleaner production methods, recycling and composting, and reducing energy consumption.

    ○ **Conserving resources:** Businesses should conserve resources by using them wisely and efficiently. This can be done by using recycled materials, water-saving appliances, and energy-efficient lighting.

    ○ **Using sustainable practices:** Businesses should use sustainable practices in their operations. This can be done by using renewable energy sources, planting trees, and reducing waste.

- **Giving back to the community:** Businesses should give back to the community by supporting local charities, sponsoring events, and volunteering their time.

    ○ **Supporting local charities:** Businesses can support local charities by donating money, goods, or services. This helps to make a difference in the lives of people in the community.

    ○ **Sponsoring events:** Businesses can sponsor events that benefit the community, such as fundraising galas or sporting events. This helps to raise awareness for important causes and generate funds for local charities.

    ○ **Volunteering their time:** Businesses can encourage their employees to volunteer their time to help others in the community. This helps to build a sense of community and make a difference in the lives of others.

- **Being transparent:** Businesses should be transparent about their activities. This includes disclosing financial information, reporting on environmental impacts, and providing information about their corporate governance practices.

- **Disclosing financial information:** Businesses should disclose their financial information to the public. This helps to ensure that investors and other stakeholders have access to accurate information about the company's financial health.
- **Reporting on environmental impacts:** Businesses should report on their environmental impacts. This helps to track the company's progress in reducing its environmental impact and to identify areas where further improvement is needed.
- **Providing information about their corporate governance practices:** Businesses should provide information about their corporate governance practices. This helps to ensure that the company is managed in a transparent and accountable manner.

- **Being accountable:** Businesses should be accountable for their decisions and actions. This means being willing to listen to feedback and to make changes when necessary.

  - **Listening to feedback:** Businesses should listen to feedback from their employees, customers, and other stakeholders. This helps to identify areas where the company can improve and to build trust with its stakeholders.
  - **Making changes when necessary:** Businesses should be willing to make changes when necessary. This means being open to new ideas and being willing to admit when the company has made a mistake.

By fulfilling their social responsibilities, businesses can create a more just and equitable society. They can help to improve the lives of others, build goodwill with their community, and create a more sustainable future.

3.3. Development and Maintenance of Interest Groups:

Interest groups are formed when people with shared interests come together to try to influence public policy. The development and maintenance of interest groups is a complex process that involves a number of factors, including:

- **The existence of a shared interest:** Interest groups are more likely to form when there is a group of people who share a common interest that they feel is not being adequately represented by the government. For example, environmental groups formed in response to concerns about air and water pollution.
- **The availability of resources:** Interest groups need resources, such as money, time, and expertise, in order to operate effectively. These resources can come from members, donors, or foundations.
- **The political opportunity structure:** The political opportunity structure refers to the set of factors that make it easier or harder for interest groups to influence public policy. For example, interest groups are more likely to be successful in influencing policy when there is a divided government or when there is a strong public demand for change.
- **The leadership of the interest group:** The leadership of an interest group plays a crucial role in its development and maintenance. Effective leaders are able to mobilize members, raise money, and develop effective strategies for influencing public policy.

Once an interest group is formed, it needs to be maintained in order to continue to be effective. This involves a number of activities, such as:

- **Recruiting and retaining members:** Interest groups need a critical mass of members in order to be effective. They need to recruit new members and retain existing members in order to maintain their influence.

- **Generating financial resources:** Interest groups need money in order to operate effectively. They need to raise money from members, donors, or foundations.
- **Advocating for their policy goals:** Interest groups need to advocate for their policy goals in order to influence public policy. They do this by lobbying elected officials, filing lawsuits, and conducting public education campaigns.
- **Building coalitions with other interest groups:** Interest groups can often be more effective when they work together with other interest groups. This is because they can pool their resources and expertise, and they can present a united front to elected officials.

The development and maintenance of interest groups is an important part of the political process. Interest groups play a key role in representing the interests of their members and in influencing public policy.

A. Business and economic interest groups

Business and economic interest groups are organizations that represent the interests of businesses and industries. They lobby government officials, file lawsuits, and conduct public education campaigns in order to influence public policy.

These groups represent a wide range of businesses and industries, from large multinational corporations to small businesses. They work to promote policies that are favorable to businesses, such as tax cuts, deregulation, and free trade.

Business and economic interest groups are often very powerful. They have a lot of money and they can hire the best lobbyists. They also have a lot of influence over elected officials, who often rely on their campaign contributions.

As a result, business and economic interest groups have a significant impact on public policy. They can often shape the debate on important issues and they can influence the outcome of legislation.

B. Economic Interest Groups:

Economic interest groups play a significant role in the political process. They have a lot of money, influence, and expertise, and they use these resources to shape public policy. As a result, they are a major force in American politics. Economic interest groups can build coalitions with other interest groups to increase their influence. This can be especially effective when the groups share common interests.

C. A business interest group

A business interest group is an organization that represents the interests of businesses and industries. They lobby government officials, file lawsuits, and conduct public education campaigns in order to influence public policy.

Some of the most well-known business interest groups in the United States include:

- The Chamber of Commerce of the United States
- The National Association of Manufacturers
- The American Petroleum Institute

These groups represent a wide range of businesses and industries, from large multinational corporations to small businesses. They work to promote policies that are favorable to businesses, such as tax cuts, deregulation, and free trade.

Business interest groups are often very powerful. They have a lot of money and they can hire the best lobbyists. They also have a lot of influence over elected officials, who often rely on their campaign contributions.

As a result, business interest groups have a significant impact on public policy. They can often shape the debate on important issues and they can influence the outcome of legislation.

D. A Labor Interest Group:

A labor interest group is an organization that represents the interests of workers. They lobby government officials, file lawsuits, and conduct public education campaigns in order to influence public policy.

These groups represent a wide range of workers, from blue-collar workers to white-collar workers. They work to promote policies that are favorable to workers, such as higher wages, better working conditions, and more job security.

Labor interest groups are often very powerful. They have a lot of members and they can raise a lot of money. They also have a lot of influence over elected officials, who often rely on their support to get elected.

As a result, labor interest groups have a significant impact on public policy. They can often shape the debate on important issues and they can influence the outcome of legislation.

D. A Professional Interest Groups:

A professional interest group is an organization that represents the interests of people who work in a particular profession. They lobby government officials, file lawsuits, and conduct public education campaigns in order to influence public policy.

These groups represent a wide range of professionals, from lawyers to doctors to teachers. They work to promote policies that are favorable to their members, such as higher salaries, better working conditions, and more professional autonomy.

E. Agricultural Interest Groups:

An agricultural interest group is an organization that represents the interests of farmers, ranchers, and other agricultural producers. They lobby government officials, file lawsuits, and conduct public education campaigns in order to influence public policy.

These groups represent a wide range of agricultural producers, from large farms to small family farms. They work to promote policies that are favorable to agriculture, such as subsidies, crop insurance, and trade protection.

F. Environmental Interest Groups:

An environmental interest group is an organization that advocates for the protection of the environment. They lobby government officials, file lawsuits, and conduct public education campaigns in order to influence public policy.

These groups represent a wide range of environmental concerns, from climate change to pollution to deforestation. They work to promote policies that protect the environment, such as clean air and water regulations, renewable energy, and sustainable development.

Environmental interest groups can file lawsuits to challenge government regulations or to block legislation that they oppose. This can be a powerful tool for influencing public policy, especially when the government is reluctant to change its position.

Environmental interest groups can conduct public education campaigns to raise awareness of environmental issues and to build support for their positions. This can be done through advertising, public relations, and grassroots organizing.

G. Consumer Interest Groups:

Consumer interest groups are organizations that advocate for the protection of consumers. They work to ensure that consumers have access to safe products and services, that they are not misled by false advertising, and that they are not taken advantage of by businesses.

These groups represent a wide range of consumer concerns, from product safety to financial protection to privacy. They work to promote policies that protect consumers, such as product recalls, truth-in-advertising laws, and consumer privacy regulations.

Consumer interest groups are often very powerful. They have a lot of members and they can raise a lot of money. They also have a lot of influence over elected officials, who often rely on their support to get elected.

As a result, consumer interest groups have a significant impact on public policy. They can often shape the debate on important issues and they can influence the outcome of legislation.

H. An Ideological Interest Groups:

An ideological interest group is an organization that promotes a particular ideology or set of beliefs. They often focus on influencing public policy, but they may also engage in other activities, such as providing education or training, or organizing protests.

These groups represent a wide range of ideologies, from liberal to conservative to libertarian. They work to promote policies that align with their beliefs, such as gun control, environmental protection, abortion rights

I. Public Interest Groups:

A public interest group is an organization that seeks to promote the common good, rather than the interests of a particular group or individual. They often focus on issues that affect a broad range of people, such as the environment, consumer protection, or civil rights.

Here are some of the characteristics of public interest groups:

- **They are non-profit organizations.** This means that they do not make a profit, and their primary goal is to promote the public good.
- **They are typically funded by donations from individuals and foundations.** This allows them to operate independently from special interests and to focus on the issues that they believe are important.
- **They have a broad membership base.** This gives them a large pool of potential supporters and volunteers, and it also helps them to build legitimacy and credibility.
- **They are often active in lobbying and advocacy.** This means that they work to influence public policy by meeting with elected officials, filing lawsuits, and conducting public education campaigns.
- **They may also engage in research and education.** This helps them to stay informed about the issues that they are

concerned about and to educate the public about these issues.

H. Single-Issue Interest Groups:

A single-issue interest group is a type of interest group that focuses on a single issue, such as abortion, gun control, or environmental protection. They often have a very narrow focus and they do not typically engage in other activities, such as lobbying or research.

Single-issue interest groups can be very effective in influencing public policy, especially on issues that are highly polarized. They can mobilize their members to contact elected officials and to vote in elections. They can also raise a lot of money to support their cause.

Here are some of the characteristics of single-issue interest groups:

- **They focus on a single issue.** This allows them to specialize in their area of expertise and to build a strong base of support among people who share their concerns.
- **They are often very passionate about their issue.** This can be a powerful motivator for members and volunteers, and it can also help to attract media attention.
- **They can be very effective at mobilizing their members.** Single-issue interest groups often have a large and active membership base, which they can use to contact elected officials, donate money, and vote in elections.
- **They can raise a lot of money.** Single-issue interest groups often have a small number of very wealthy donors, who are willing to contribute large sums of money to support their cause.

3.3.2. Influence Of Interest Groups On Government:

Interest groups can also influence government by shaping public opinion. They can do this by conducting public education campaigns, publishing research, and issuing press releases. When the public is aware of an issue and supports a particular policy, it is more likely that elected officials will support that policy as well.

Interest groups play an important role in American democracy. They help to ensure that the voices of ordinary citizens are heard in the political process. They also help to hold elected officials accountable and to ensure that government policies serve the public interest. However, interest groups can also be a source of corruption and undue influence. It is important to be aware of the influence of interest groups and to hold them accountable for their actions.

3.3.3. Government Protection Policies Against The Illegal Business Practice:

Governments have a number of policies in place to protect businesses from illegal practices. These policies include:

- **Antitrust laws:** Antitrust laws prohibit businesses from engaging in anti-competitive practices, such as price-fixing, collusion, and monopolization. These laws are designed to protect consumers from businesses that are able to charge excessive prices or control the market for a particular product or service.
- **Consumer protection laws:** Consumer protection laws protect consumers from unfair or deceptive business practices. These laws prohibit businesses from making false or misleading claims about their products or services, from engaging in bait-and-switch tactics, or from failing to disclose important information to consumers.
- **Environmental protection laws:** Environmental protection

laws protect the environment from pollution and other forms of environmental harm. These laws prohibit businesses from discharging pollutants into the air or water, from dumping hazardous waste, or from destroying endangered species.

- **Labor laws:** Labor laws protect workers from exploitation and abuse. These laws prohibit businesses from discriminating against workers on the basis of race, sex, religion, or national origin, from paying workers less than minimum wage, or from requiring workers to work in unsafe or unhealthy conditions.

These are just a few of the policies that governments have in place to protect businesses from illegal practices. These policies are designed to ensure that businesses compete fairly, that consumers are protected from fraud and deception, that the environment is protected from pollution, and that workers are treated fairly.

3.3.4 Unfair Trade Practices

Unfair trade practices (UTPs) are business practices that are considered deceptive, fraudulent, or otherwise unethical. They can harm consumers, businesses, and the overall economy.

There are many different types of UTPs, but some of the most common include:

- **False advertising:** This is the act of making false or misleading statements about a product or service. For example, a company might advertise that its product is "natural" when it is actually made with synthetic ingredients.
- **Deceptive pricing:** This is the act of pricing a product or service in a way that is misleading to consumers. For example, a company might advertise a product as being "on sale" when

> the sale price is actually higher than the regular price.

- **Bait-and-switch:** This is the act of advertising a product or service at a low price, but then refusing to sell it at that price or substituting a different product or service. For example, a company might advertise a TV for $100, but then tell customers that the TV is out of stock and offer them a more expensive TV instead.

- **Unfair contract terms:** These are terms in a contract that are unfairly favorable to one party, usually the business. For example, a contract might have a term that allows the business to cancel the contract at any time, but does not allow the consumer to cancel the contract.

- **Tying arrangements:** This is the practice of requiring a customer to buy one product or service in order to buy another product or service. For example, a company might require a customer to buy a printer in order to buy ink cartridges for the printer.

UTPs can be harmful to consumers in a number of ways. They can mislead consumers about the quality or features of a product or service, leading them to make poor purchasing decisions. They can also make it difficult for consumers to compare prices and find the best deals.

UTPs can also be harmful to businesses. They can create unfair competition and make it difficult for businesses to succeed. They can also damage the reputation of a business and make it difficult to attract customers.

The laws governing UTPs vary from country to country. In the United States, the Federal Trade Commission (FTC) is responsible for enforcing the laws against UTPs. The FTC has a broad authority to investigate and take action against businesses that engage in UTPs.

If you believe that you have been the victim of an unfair trade practice, you should contact the FTC or your local consumer protection agency. You may also be able to file a lawsuit against the business that engaged in the unfair trade practice.

3.3.5. Realtioship Management Skills

CRM stands for Customer Relationship Management. It is a business strategy that focuses on managing all aspects of a customer's relationship with a company, from sales and marketing to customer service and support.

1. The First Step In CRM Is Understanding The Customer's Needs.

The first step in CRM is understanding the customer's needs. This can be done by collecting data about the customer, such as their demographics, purchase history, and contact information. This data can be used to create customer profiles, which can help businesses to better understand the needs of their customers.

Once the customer's needs are understood, businesses can then develop strategies to meet those needs. This might involve offering products or services that are tailored to the customer's specific needs, or providing personalized customer service.

By understanding the customer's needs and developing strategies to meet those needs, businesses can build strong relationships with their customers. This can lead to increased sales, improved customer satisfaction, and increased customer loyalty.

2. Treating People As Individuals

Treating people as individuals means seeing and respecting them as unique and distinct beings, with their own thoughts, feelings, experiences, and perspectives. It means not making assumptions about them based on their race, gender, age, religion, or any other group affiliation. It means listening to them with an open mind and heart, and trying to understand their point of view. It means being respectful of their differences, and not judging them.

There are many benefits to treating people as individuals. It can help to build stronger relationships, create a more inclusive and welcoming environment, and promote understanding and acceptance. It can also help to reduce prejudice and discrimination.

3. Under Promise And Over Deliver

The phrase "under promise and over deliver" means to set realistic expectations and then exceed them. This is a strategy that can be used in many different contexts, including business, personal relationships, and even everyday life.

When you under promise, you are setting expectations that are lower than what you are actually capable of achieving. This can be a good thing because it can help to avoid disappointment. If you promise too much, and then you are unable to deliver, people will be disappointed. But if you under promise, and then you exceed expectations, people will be pleasantly surprised.

Over delivering means going above and beyond what is expected of you. This can be done by doing something extra, or by doing something in a way that is unexpected and appreciated. When you over deliver, you are showing that you care about the person or people you are dealing with, and that you are willing to go the extra mile.

The "under promise and over deliver" strategy can be a very effective way to build trust and rapport with others. When people know that you are someone who can be counted on to deliver, they are more likely to do business with you, or to have a positive relationship with you.

4. Know Yourself and Manage Yourself:

Knowing yourself and managing yourself are two essential skills that can help you achieve your goals and live a fulfilling life.

Knowing yourself means understanding your strengths and weaknesses, your values and goals, and your emotional triggers. It also means understanding your learning style and how you best work and communicate. When you know yourself, you are better able to set realistic goals, make informed decisions, and manage your time and energy effectively.

Managing yourself means taking responsibility for your own actions and choices. It means setting goals and creating a plan to achieve them, setting boundaries, and managing your time and stress levels. It also means being aware of your emotions and how they affect your behavior, and taking steps to manage them in a healthy way.

3.3.6. Relationship Management Actives:

Relationship management activities are the actions taken to build, maintain, and strengthen relationships with customers, clients, partners, and other stakeholders. These activities can be formal or informal, and they can take place in person, over the phone, or online.

1. Social Media Connectivity:

Social media connectivity refers to the ability of people to connect with each other through social media platforms. This can be done by sharing posts, liking and commenting on posts, following each other, and joining groups and communities. Social media connectivity can be used to stay in touch with friends and family, build relationships with colleagues and business partners, and connect with people who share similar interests. Social media connectivity can be a powerful tool for connecting with people and building relationships. However, it is important to use social media responsibly. People should be careful about the information that they share on social media, and they should be aware of the risks of cyberbullying and online predators.

2. Give Adequate Training To Emplyees:

Adequate training for employees means providing them with the knowledge and skills they need to do their jobs effectively. This includes training on the company's products and services, its policies and procedures, and the specific tasks and duties of their job. The best way to provide adequate training for employees will vary depending on the specific needs of the company and the employees. However, all employers should make a commitment to providing their employees with the training they need to be successful.

3. Opt-in email Marketing Tools:

Opt-in email marketing is a marketing strategy where businesses only send emails to people who have explicitly opted in to receive them. This means that the recipient has given their consent to receive emails from the business, and is therefore more likely to be interested in what the business has to say. Opt-in email marketing can be a powerful tool for relationship management. By building a list of subscribers who have opted in to receive emails, businesses can stay in touch with their customers and prospects, and build relationships with them over time.

4. Membership Card:

A membership card is a physical or digital card that gives the holder certain benefits, such as discounts, exclusive content, or early access to events. Membership cards can be a valuable tool for businesses to improve relationship management with their customers. Overall, membership cards can be a valuable tool for businesses to improve relationship management with their customers. By collecting customer data, rewarding loyalty, personalizing the experience, gathering feedback, and tracking customer behavior, businesses can use membership cards to build stronger relationships with their customers and to grow their business.

3.3.7. Relationship Management Structure:

A relationship management structure is a framework that defines how an organization manages its relationships with its customers, partners, and other stakeholders. It typically includes the roles and responsibilities of different departments or teams, as well as the processes and tools used to manage relationships. There are many different types of relationship management structures, and the best structure for an organization will vary depending on its size, industry, and customer base.

1. Richard White's Study:

Richard White's study, "Organizational Design and Ethics: The Effects of Rigid Hierarchy on Moral Reasoning," investigates the relationship between hierarchical institutional systems and their effects on the moral growth of organizational stakeholders.

White argues that rigid hierarchies can restrict the moral development of organizational members by limiting their opportunities for autonomy and moral agency. In a rigid hierarchy, power is concentrated at the top of the organization, and lower-level members are often subject to the authority of their superiors. This can lead to a situation where lower-level members feel like they have no control over their own work, and that their moral decisions are being made for them by others.

White's study found that members of organizations with rigid hierarchies were more likely to make unethical decisions than members of organizations with flatter hierarchies. This is because members of rigid hierarchies are less likely to feel responsible for the consequences of their actions, and they are more likely to defer to the authority of their superiors.

White's study has implications for the design of organizations. Organizations that want to promote moral growth among their members should avoid rigid hierarchies and create structures that give all members a voice and a sense of responsibility.

2. Schminke Study:

The Schmink study is a research study that investigated the relationship between ethical climate and ethical decision-making. The study was conducted by Dr. Judith Schmink, a professor of management at the University of Wisconsin-Milwaukee.

The study found that ethical climate, which is the shared perceptions of what is considered ethical behavior in an organization, has a significant impact on ethical decision-making. In organizations with strong ethical climates, employees are more likely to make ethical decisions, even when they are faced with pressure to do otherwise.

The study found that the personal moral philosophy dimension had the strongest impact on ethical decision-making. However, the organizational moral values and organizational structure and systems dimensions also played a significant role. The Schmink study has implications for organizations. Organizations that want to promote ethical decision-making should create a strong ethical climate.

3.4. Government Policies Promoting Economic Interest:

Government Policies Promoting Economic Interest may involve a wide range of initiatives, from infrastructure investment to education reform. The specific economic development policies that are implemented will vary depending on the country's specific needs and goals. The success of economic development policies depends on a number of factors, including the quality of implementation, the overall economic climate, and the availability of resources.

(i). Macroeconomic Stability

Macroeconomic stability is a condition in which the major economic variables, such as inflation, unemployment, and economic growth, are relatively stable. This means that there is not a lot of volatility in these variables, which can help to create an environment that is conducive to economic growth and prosperity.

There are a number of factors that can contribute to macroeconomic stability, including:

- **Fiscal policy:** Fiscal policy refers to the government's spending and taxation decisions. When the government runs a balanced budget or a surplus, it helps to stabilize the economy.
- **Monetary policy:** Monetary policy refers to the central bank's control of the money supply and interest rates. When the central bank implements sound monetary policy, it can help to keep inflation under control.
- **Exchange rate policy:** Exchange rate policy refers to the government's control of the exchange rate. A stable exchange rate can help to reduce uncertainty and volatility in the economy.
- **Structural reforms:** Structural reforms refer to changes to the economy that can improve its efficiency and productivity. These reforms can include things like deregulation, privatization, and trade liberalization.

Macroeconomic stability is important for a number of reasons. First, it can help to promote economic growth. When the economy is stable, businesses are more likely to invest and hire new workers. This can lead to higher economic growth.

(ii). Less Restrictive Regulation And Tackle Corruption:

Less restrictive regulation and tackling corruption are two important pillars of economic development.

Less restrictive regulation can help to promote economic growth by reducing the costs of doing business. When businesses have to comply with fewer regulations, they can save money and invest more in their operations. This can lead to higher productivity and economic growth.

Tackling corruption can also help to promote economic growth by reducing the uncertainty and risk associated with doing business. When businesses are not worried about corruption, they are more likely to invest and hire new workers. This can lead to higher economic growth.

There are a number of ways to achieve less restrictive regulation and tackle corruption. Some of these ways include:

- **Simplifying the regulatory framework:** This can be done by reducing the number of regulations, streamlining the approval process, and making regulations more transparent.
- **Making regulations more flexible:** This can be done by allowing businesses to choose the regulations that are most appropriate for their operations.
- **Enforcing regulations fairly and consistently:** This can help to deter corruption and ensure that businesses are treated fairly.
- **Creating a culture of transparency and accountability:** This can be done by publishing information about regulations and enforcement actions, and by making it easy

for businesses to report corruption.

By taking these steps, countries can help to achieve less restrictive regulation and tackle corruption, which can lay the foundation for long-term economic growth and prosperity.

(iii). Privatization and Deregulation:

Privatization and deregulation are two economic policies that are often implemented together. Privatization refers to the transfer of ownership of a public enterprise to the private sector. Deregulation refers to the removal of government restrictions on economic activity.

Privatization can be done in a number of ways, including:

- **Sale of government assets:** The government can sell its assets, such as factories, mines, and utilities, to private investors.
- **Concessions:** The government can grant concessions to private companies to operate public services, such as prisons, schools, and hospitals.
- **Public-private partnerships:** The government can partner with private companies to finance and operate public services.

Deregulation can be done in a number of ways, including:

- **Removal of price controls:** The government can remove price controls on goods and services, such as gasoline and electricity.
- **Reduction of licensing requirements:** The government can reduce the number of licenses required to start a business.
- **Streamlining of regulations:** The government can

streamline regulations, making them easier to understand and comply with.

Privatization and deregulation are often motivated by the belief that they will lead to economic efficiency and growth. Proponents of these policies argue that private businesses are more efficient than government-owned businesses and that deregulation will reduce the costs of doing business.

(iv). An effective tax structure is one that is fair, efficient, and easy to administer.

It should be fair in the sense that it should be based on the ability to pay. It should be efficient in the sense that it should minimize the administrative costs of collecting taxes. And it should be easy to administer in the sense that it should be easy for taxpayers to understand and comply with.

There are a number of factors that can contribute to an effective tax structure, including:

- **A broad base of taxation:** A broad base of taxation means that a large number of people and businesses are subject to taxation. This helps to ensure that the tax burden is shared fairly.
- **Low marginal tax rates:** Marginal tax rates are the rates at which taxpayers pay additional taxes on their income. Low marginal tax rates encourage people to work and invest, which can lead to economic growth.
- **Simple tax laws:** Simple tax laws are easier for taxpayers to understand and comply with. This can help to reduce compliance costs and improve voluntary compliance.
- **Effective enforcement:** Effective enforcement means that

the government has the resources and the will to collect taxes from taxpayers who do not comply. This helps to ensure that everyone pays their fair share of taxes.

Tax collection is the process of collecting taxes from taxpayers. It is an important part of any tax system. Effective tax collection is essential for ensuring that the government has the resources it needs to provide essential services and to maintain a sound financial position.

(V). Investment In Public Services:

Investment in public services is the allocation of government resources to provide essential services to the public, such as education, healthcare, transportation, and infrastructure. These services are important for the well-being of the population and for the economic development of the country.

There are many benefits to investing in public services. These benefits include:

- **Improved quality of life:** Public services can improve the quality of life for people by providing them with access to essential goods and services. For example, education can help people to get better jobs, healthcare can help people to stay healthy, and transportation can help people to get around.
- **Increased economic growth:** Public services can help to increase economic growth by providing a skilled workforce, a healthy population, and a well-functioning infrastructure. For example, education can help to create a skilled workforce, healthcare can help to keep people healthy, and infrastructure can help to move goods and people around.
- **Reduced inequality:** Public services can help to reduce inequality by providing essential services to everyone,

regardless of their income or social status. For example, education can help to provide everyone with the opportunity to succeed, and healthcare can help to ensure that everyone has access to quality care.

- **Strengthened social cohesion:** Public services can help to strengthen social cohesion by bringing people together and creating a sense of community. For example, education can help to create a shared sense of values and identity, and healthcare can help to connect people to their communities.

(vi). Diversification Away From Agriculture:

Diversification away from agriculture refers to the practice of farmers shifting their focus away from traditional agricultural activities and towards other income-generating activities. There are many reasons why farmers might choose to diversify away from agriculture. Some of the most common reasons include:

- To reduce risk: Agriculture is a risky business, and diversification can help to spread risk by providing farmers with a more diversified income stream.
- To increase income: Non-farm activities can often generate higher incomes than traditional agricultural activities.
- To improve quality of life: Diversification can allow farmers to have more flexibility in their work schedule and to pursue other interests.
- To adapt to climate change: Climate change is posing a major challenge to agriculture, and diversification can help farmers to adapt to these challenges by diversifying their crops and livestock, and by investing in new technologies.

Chapter 4. Environmental and Consumer Ethical Issues

4.1. Environmental Ethics

Environmental ethics is a branch of ethics that considers the moral relationship of human beings to the environment. It is a relatively new field of study, having emerged in the 1970s in response to the growing awareness of environmental problems such as pollution, deforestation, and climate change.

Environmental ethics seeks to answer questions such as:

- What is the value of the environment?
- Do non-human beings have moral standing?
- What are our moral obligations to the environment?
- How can we live in a more sustainable way?

There are two main schools of thought in environmental ethics: anthropocentrism and non-anthropocentrism.

- **Anthropocentrism** is the view that only humans have moral standing. This means that the only things that matter morally are things that affect humans. From an anthropocentric perspective, the environment only has value insofar as it is useful to humans.
- **Non-anthropocentrism** is the view that non-human beings also have moral standing. This means that we have moral obligations to other living things, such as animals, plants, and ecosystems. Non-anthropocentric theories can be divided into two main types: biocentrism and ecocentrism.
    - **Biocentrism** is the view that all living things have intrinsic value. This means that they have value in and of themselves, regardless of their usefulness to humans.
    - **Ecocentrism** is the view that ecosystems have intrinsic value. This means that they have value in and of themselves,

regardless of the value of the individual organisms that make them up.

Environmental ethics is a complex and evolving field. There is no single answer to the question of what our moral obligations to the environment are. However, environmental ethics can provide us with a framework for thinking about these issues and making decisions that are more ethical and sustainable.

4.2. Environmental Sustainability

Environmental sustainability is the practice of using natural resources in a way that meets the needs of the present without compromising the ability of future generations to meet their own needs. It is about finding ways to live and work that protect the environment and natural resources for future generations.

The main features of environmental sustainability include:

- **Conservation of natural resources:** This includes using resources efficiently, reducing waste, and recycling.
- **Protection of ecosystems:** This includes preventing pollution, conserving biodiversity, and restoring damaged ecosystems.
- **Sustainable development:** This means promoting economic growth that does not harm the environment.

There are three main pillars of environmental sustainability:

- **Economic viability:** This means ensuring that businesses and communities can thrive without harming the environment.
- **Environmental protection:** This means protecting the air, water, land, and biodiversity.

- **Social equity:** This means ensuring that everyone has access to clean air, water, and a healthy environment.

Environmental sustainability is important because it is essential for the health and well-being of people and the planet. It can help to mitigate climate change, reduce pollution, and protect biodiversity. It can also help to create jobs and boost economic growth.

4.3. Environmental Ethics And Human Values

Environmental ethics is the branch of ethics that studies the moral relationship of human beings to the environment and to other living things. It is concerned with how we should interact with the natural world, and how we should value it.

Human values are the things that are important to individuals and societies. They can be religious, cultural, or personal. They can also be based on our understanding of the natural world.

Environmental ethics and human values are closely intertwined. Our values influence how we view the environment, and our interactions with the environment shape our values.

There are many different ways to apply environmental ethics to human values. Some people believe that we should live in harmony with nature, while others believe that we should use the environment to meet our needs, but do so sustainably. Some people believe that we should protect all forms of life, while others believe that we should prioritize the well-being of humans.

The debate over environmental ethics is complex and there is no easy answer. However, it is an important debate to have, as our choices about how to interact with the environment will have a profound impact on the future of our planet.

Here are some specific examples of how human values can influence our environmental ethics:

- **The value of beauty:** Many people value the beauty of nature. This value can lead us to want to protect natural areas, such as forests and mountains.
- **The value of health:** We value our health, and we know that the environment can affect our health. This value can lead us to want to protect clean air and water, and to reduce pollution.
- **The value of tradition:** Some people value traditional ways of life that are connected to the land. This value can lead us to want to protect traditional cultures and practices.
- **The value of future generations:** We value the well-being of future generations. This value can lead us to want to take steps to protect the environment for future generations.

Ultimately, the way we value the environment is a reflection of our own values. By understanding our values, we can better understand our environmental ethics and make choices that are in line with those ethics.

4.3.1. Importance of Environmental Ethics

Environmental ethics is important because it provides a moral framework for how humans interact with the natural environment. It helps us consider the effects our actions have on the planet and guides us in making more ethical and sustainable decisions.

Here are some of the specific importances of environmental ethics:

- **Protecting the environment and natural resources:**

Environmental ethics can help us to address environmental problems, such as pollution, deforestation, and climate change. It can also help us to develop ways to live in harmony with nature that can protect the environment for future generations.

- **Promoting biodiversity and wildlife conservation:**

Environmental ethics can help us to understand the importance of biodiversity and the need to protect endangered species. It can also guide us in making decisions about how to use natural resources in a way that minimizes harm to wildlife.

- **Encouraging sustainable development:**

Environmental ethics can help us to create a more sustainable future by promoting practices that conserve resources, reduce pollution, and protect the environment.

- **Building a better relationship with nature:**

Environmental ethics can help us to appreciate the value of nature and to see ourselves as part of a larger ecosystem. It can also help us to develop a sense of responsibility for the environment and to make choices that benefit all living things.

Environmental ethics is a complex and ever-changing field, but it is essential for our time. As we face the challenges of climate change, pollution, and other environmental problems, we need to draw on the insights of environmental ethics to find solutions that are both ethical and sustainable. We can all make a difference in protecting the environment by making small changes in our daily lives. Environmental ethics can help us do this by providing us with a moral compass and by helping us make more ethical and sustainable choices.

4.3.2. Causes of Environmental Problem

Some of the major causes of environmental problems:

- **Pollution:** Pollution is the introduction of harmful substances or contaminants into the environment. It can come from a variety of sources, including industrial emissions, agricultural runoff, and motor vehicles. Pollution can have a significant impact on the environment, causing air, water, and soil pollution, as well as noise pollution.
- **Overpopulation:** Overpopulation is the state of having a population that is too large for the available resources. It can lead to environmental problems such as deforestation, water scarcity, and climate change.
- **Deforestation:** Deforestation is the clearing of forests for human use. It can lead to a number of environmental problems, including soil erosion, water pollution, and climate change.
- **Climate change:** Climate change is the long-term alteration of temperature and typical weather patterns in a place. It is caused by human activities, such as the burning of fossil fuels, which release greenhouse gases into the atmosphere. Greenhouse gases trap heat, causing the Earth's temperature to rise. Climate change can have a significant impact on the environment, causing sea level rise, extreme weather events, and changes in plant and animal life.
- **Waste disposal:** Waste disposal is the process of getting rid of trash and other waste materials. It can be a major

environmental problem, as improper waste disposal can pollute the environment.

- **Overconsumption:** Overconsumption is the act of consuming more goods and services than is necessary. It can lead to environmental problems such as resource depletion and pollution.

These are just some of the major causes of environmental problems. There are many other factors that can contribute to environmental degradation, such as poverty, inequality, and lack of education. It is important to understand the causes of environmental problems in order to develop solutions that can address them effectively.

4.4. Meaning of Values

Values are the beliefs and principles that are important to us. They guide our thoughts, feelings, and actions. Values can be about anything, but they often relate to things like honesty, integrity, compassion, and respect.

Values are important because they help us to live a meaningful and fulfilling life. They provide us with a sense of purpose and direction. They also help us to make decisions and to resolve conflicts.

4.4.1. Needs of Human Values

Some of the specific needs of human values:

- **To create a just and equitable society:** Human values such as fairness, equality, and respect are essential for creating a just and equitable society. These values help to ensure that everyone is treated fairly and with dignity, regardless of their race, religion, gender, or social status.
- **To build strong relationships:** Human values such as trust,

honesty, and compassion are essential for building strong relationships. These values help us to connect with others on a deep level and to create lasting bonds of friendship and love.

- **To make good decisions:** Human values such as wisdom, courage, and responsibility help us to make good decisions in life. These values help us to weigh the consequences of our actions and to make choices that are in our best interests and the best interests of others.

- **To live a meaningful life:** Human values such as purpose, hope, and gratitude help us to live a meaningful life. These values give us a sense of direction and purpose in life, and they help us to appreciate the good things in our lives.

The needs of human values are endless. They are essential for living a good and fulfilling life, and they are the foundation of a just and equitable society.

4.4.2. Characteristics of Human Values

Human values are the principles that guide our thoughts, actions, and relationships. They are essential for living a good and fulfilling life.

Here are 15 characteristics of human values:

1. **Universal:** Human values are universally applicable, meaning that they are important for everyone, regardless of their culture, religion, or background.

2. **Transcendent:** Human values are timeless and enduring, meaning that they are still important today as they were in the past and will be in the future.

3. **Relative:** Human values are relative, meaning that they may be interpreted differently by different people. However, there are some core values that are generally agreed upon, such as

honesty, respect, and compassion.

4. **Dynamic:** Human values are dynamic, meaning that they can change over time. This is because they are influenced by the culture, society, and historical context in which they exist.

5. **Integrative:** Human values are integrative, meaning that they are interconnected and interdependent. This means that they cannot be separated from each other and that they all play a role in creating a good and just society.

6. **Fundamental:** Human values are fundamental to our sense of right and wrong, and they provide us with a framework for making decisions and living our lives.

7. **Motivational:** Human values are motivational, meaning that they can motivate us to act in certain ways. For example, the value of honesty can motivate us to tell the truth, even when it is difficult.

8. **Emotional:** Human values can evoke strong emotions, such as love, compassion, and anger. These emotions can motivate us to act in accordance with our values.

9. **Cognitive:** Human values can also be cognitive, meaning that we can think about them and reflect on them. This can help us to understand our values and to make better decisions about how to live our lives.

10. **Behavioral:** Human values can also be behavioral, meaning that we can act in accordance with them. This is how we express our values to others and to the world.

11. **Social:** Human values are social, meaning that they are shared by groups of people. This is why they are important for creating a cohesive and harmonious society.

12. **Cultural:** Human values are also cultural, meaning that they are influenced by the culture in which we live. This is why there is some variation in values from culture to culture.

13. **Personal:** Human values are also personal, meaning that they

are unique to each individual. This is why we all have different priorities and different ways of expressing our values.

14. **Dynamic:** Human values are dynamic, meaning that they can change over time. This is because we are constantly learning and growing, and our values can change as a result.

15. **Evolving:** Human values are evolving, meaning that they are constantly being reinterpreted and re-evaluated. This is because the world is constantly changing, and our values need to change with it.

These are just some of the characteristics of human values. By understanding these characteristics, we can better understand the role that values play in our lives and in society.

4.4.3. Intrinsic And Extrinsic Human Values

Intrinsic and extrinsic values are two types of values that people hold. Intrinsic values are those that are valuable in and of themselves, while extrinsic values are those that are valuable because they lead to something else.

Here are some examples of intrinsic values:

- **Honesty:** Being honest is valuable because it is the right thing to do, regardless of the consequences.
- **Compassion:** Compassion is valuable because it allows us to connect with others and to feel empathy for their suffering.
- **Courage:** Courage is valuable because it allows us to stand up for what we believe in, even when it is difficult.
- **Love:** Love is valuable because it is a deep and abiding feeling of affection and care for another person.
- **Peace:** Peace is valuable because it is the absence of war and

conflict.

Here are some examples of extrinsic values:

- **Money:** Money is valuable because it can be used to buy things that we need or want.
- **Power:** Power is valuable because it can be used to influence others and to get what we want.
- **Status:** Status is valuable because it can be used to gain respect and admiration from others.
- **Beauty:** Beauty is valuable because it can be pleasing to the eye and to the senses.
- **Success:** Success is valuable because it can be seen as a measure of our worth and achievement.

It is important to note that intrinsic and extrinsic values are not mutually exclusive. For example, we may value honesty because it is the right thing to do, but we may also value honesty because it can lead to other things, such as trust and respect.

Ultimately, the relative importance of intrinsic and extrinsic values is a matter of personal opinion. However, it is important to be aware of the difference between these two types of values in order to make informed decisions about our lives.

Here are some of the key differences between intrinsic and extrinsic values:

- Intrinsic values are valuable in and of themselves, while extrinsic values are valuable because they lead to something else.
- Intrinsic values are often more enduring than extrinsic values.
- Intrinsic values are often more difficult to achieve than

extrinsic values.

- Intrinsic values are often more satisfying than extrinsic values.

It is important to note that these are just generalizations, and there are always exceptions. For example, some people may find that extrinsic values, such as money or power, are more important to them than intrinsic values. Ultimately, the relative importance of intrinsic and extrinsic values is a matter of personal opinion.

Here are some of the benefits of focusing on intrinsic values:

- **Increased happiness and well-being:** Studies have shown that people who focus on intrinsic values tend to be happier and more satisfied with their lives.
- **Stronger relationships:** Intrinsic values can help us to build stronger relationships with others by promoting trust, compassion, and respect.
- **Greater sense of purpose:** Intrinsic values can give us a greater sense of purpose in life, which can help us to feel more fulfilled.
- **Improved decision-making:** When we focus on intrinsic values, we are more likely to make decisions that are in line with our core beliefs and values.
- **Increased resilience:** Intrinsic values can help us to cope with challenges and setbacks in life.

If you want to focus more on intrinsic values in your life, here are some tips:

- **Identify your core values:** Take some time to reflect on what is important to you and what you value most in life.
- **Make choices that align with your values:** When you are

faced with a decision, ask yourself if it is in line with your core values.

- **Surround yourself with positive people:** The people you spend time with can have a big impact on your values. Make an effort to surround yourself with people who share your values.
- **Give back to others:** Helping others is a great way to connect with your intrinsic values of compassion and kindness.
- **Spend time in nature:** Nature can help us to reconnect with our values and appreciate the simple things in life.

Ultimately, the decision of whether to focus on intrinsic or extrinsic values is a personal one. However, by understanding the difference between these two types of values, you can make more informed decisions about your life and live a more fulfilling life.

4.4.3. Terminal and Instrumental Types of Human Values

Terminal and instrumental values are two types of human values that are often distinguished from each other. Terminal values are the end-states of existence that we strive for, while instrumental values are the means by which we achieve our terminal values.

Terminal values are the goals or end-states that we strive for in life. They are the things that we believe are important and worthwhile. Some examples of terminal values include:

- **Happiness:** The state of being happy and content.
- **Freedom:** The state of being free from constraints and limitations.
- **Love:** The feeling of deep affection and care for another person.

- **Peace:** The absence of war and conflict.
- **Respect:** The esteem in which we hold others.

Instrumental values are the means by which we achieve our terminal values. They are the qualities or characteristics that we believe are important in helping us to achieve our goals. Some examples of instrumental values include:

- **Honesty:** The quality of being truthful and sincere.
- **Integrity:** The quality of being honest and consistent in our thoughts, words, and actions.
- **Responsibility:** The quality of taking ownership of our actions and the consequences of those actions.
- **Compassion:** The quality of feeling empathy for others and wanting to help them.
- **Courage:** The quality of facing our fears and doing what is right, even when it is difficult.

Terminal and instrumental values are often interrelated. For example, we may believe that happiness is a terminal value, and that honesty is an instrumental value that can help us to achieve happiness.

The relative importance of terminal and instrumental values can vary from person to person. Some people may place a greater emphasis on terminal values, while others may place a greater emphasis on instrumental values. There is no right or wrong answer, and it is up to each individual to decide what is most important to them.

It is also important to note that terminal and instrumental values can change over time. As we grow and mature, our values may change as well. This is because our experiences and our understanding of the world can change over time.

Overall, terminal and instrumental values are two important concepts that can help us to understand our own values and the values of others. By understanding these concepts, we can better understand our motivations and our actions.

4.5. Environmental Legislation

Environmental legislation is a set of laws, regulations, and policies that are designed to protect the environment. These laws can be national, state, or local, and they can cover a wide range of environmental issues, such as air pollution, water pollution, and waste disposal.

The goal of environmental legislation is to prevent or reduce environmental damage and to promote sustainable development. . Environmental legislation can take many forms, including:

- **Emissions standards:** These standards set limits on the amount of pollutants that can be released into the air or water.
- **Waste disposal regulations:** These regulations govern the way that waste is generated, transported, stored, and disposed of.
- **Land use planning:** This type of regulation controls how land can be used, in order to protect sensitive areas and promote sustainable development.
- **Environmental impact assessments:** These assessments are required for major projects, such as construction or development, to assess the potential environmental impacts of the project.
- **Enforcement mechanisms:** These mechanisms are used to ensure that environmental laws are complied with, such as fines, penalties, and criminal prosecution.

Environmental legislation is an important tool for protecting the environment and promoting sustainable development. However, it is important to note that environmental legislation is not always effective. There are a number of challenges to enforcing environmental laws, such as lack of resources, corruption, and political opposition.

A. Some of the significant environmental protection regulations are as follows

(i). The Wildlife (Protection) Act, 1972:

The Wildlife (Protection) Act, 1972 is an Act of the Parliament of India enacted for the protection of plants and animal species. It was enacted in response to the declining wildlife population in India, and it is one of the most comprehensive wildlife protection laws in the world.

The Act provides for the protection of all wild animals, birds, and plants, including those that are not considered to be endangered or threatened. It also provides for the establishment of national parks, sanctuaries, and zoological parks.

The Act prohibits the hunting, killing, capturing, trading, and possession of wild animals and plants without a permit. It also prohibits the destruction of their habitats.

The Act provides for the establishment of the National Board for Wildlife and the State Boards for Wildlife to oversee the implementation of the Act.

The Act has been amended several times since it was enacted, and it is currently one of the most important laws for protecting wildlife in India.

Here are some of the key provisions of the Wildlife (Protection) Act, 1972:

- The Act classifies wild animals into two categories: Schedule I and Schedule II. Schedule I animals are those that are considered to be endangered or threatened, and they are afforded the highest level of protection. Schedule II animals are those that are not considered to be endangered or threatened, but they are still protected.
- The Act prohibits the hunting, killing, capturing, trading, and possession of wild animals and plants without a permit.
- The Act establishes national parks, sanctuaries, and zoological parks, which are areas where wild animals are protected from human disturbance.
- The Act provides for the establishment of the National Board for Wildlife and the State Boards for Wildlife to oversee the implementation of the Act.

(ii) The Water (Prevention and Control of Pollution) Act, 1974

The Water (Prevention and Control of Pollution) Act, 1974 is an Act of the Parliament of India enacted to prevent and control water pollution. It is one of the most important environmental laws in India.

The Act establishes the Central Pollution Control Board (CPCB) and State Pollution Control Boards (SPCBs) to oversee the implementation of the Act. The CPCB is responsible for coordinating the activities of the SPCBs and for providing technical assistance to them.

The Act prohibits the discharge of any pollutant into a water body without a permit from the SPCB. The SPCBs can also take measures to prevent and control water pollution, such as issuing directions to industries and other polluters, and taking legal action against them.

The Act has been amended several times since it was enacted, and it is currently one of the most important laws for preventing and controlling water pollution in India.

Here are some of the key provisions of the Water (Prevention and Control of Pollution) Act, 1974:

- The Act defines water pollution as the presence of any poisonous, noxious or polluting matter in water.
- The Act prohibits the discharge of any pollutant into a water body without a permit from the SPCB.
- The SPCBs can take measures to prevent and control water pollution, such as issuing directions to industries and other polluters, and taking legal action against them.
- The Act provides for the establishment of laboratories to test the quality of water.
- The Act provides for the establishment of a water quality monitoring network.
- The Act provides for the education and training of people in water pollution control.

(iii). The Forest (Conservation) Act, 1980:

The Forest (Conservation) Act, 1980 is an Act of the Parliament of India enacted to provide for the conservation of forests and for matters connected therewith or ancillary or incidental thereto. It was enacted in response to the increasing deforestation in India, and it is one of the most important environmental laws in India.

The Act prohibits the diversion of forest land for non-forest purposes without the prior approval of the central government. The central government can grant permission for diversion of forest land only if it is satisfied that the proposed diversion is in the public interest and that there is no alternative land available for the proposed purpose.

The Act also prohibits the felling of trees in forests without a permit from the state government. The state government can grant a permit for felling of trees only if it is satisfied that the proposed felling is necessary for bona fide agricultural or horticultural purposes, or for the development of infrastructure or for any other essential purpose.

The Act provides for the establishment of an Advisory Committee to advise the central government on matters relating to the conservation of forests. The Committee is composed of experts in the field of forestry, wildlife, and environmental protection.

The Act has been amended several times since it was enacted, and it is currently one of the most important laws for conserving forests in India.

Here are some of the key provisions of the Forest (Conservation) Act, 1980:

- The Act prohibits the diversion of forest land for non-forest purposes without the prior approval of the central government.
- The Act prohibits the felling of trees in forests without a permit from the state government.
- The Act provides for the establishment of an Advisory Committee to advise the central government on matters relating to the conservation of forests.
- The Act provides for the punishment of persons who violate the provisions of the Act.

(iv) The Air (Prevention sand Control of Pollution) Act, 1981:

The Air (Prevention and Control of Pollution) Act, 1981 is an Act of the Parliament of India enacted to provide for the prevention, control and abatement of air pollution. It is one of the most important environmental laws in India.

The Act establishes the Central Pollution Control Board (CPCB) and State Pollution Control Boards (SPCBs) to oversee the implementation of the Act. The CPCB is responsible for coordinating the activities of the SPCBs and for providing technical assistance to them.

The Act prohibits the emission of any air pollutant from any source without a permit from the SPCB. The SPCBs can also take measures to prevent and control air pollution, such as issuing directions to industries and other polluters, and taking legal action against them.

The Act has been amended several times since it was enacted, and it is currently one of the most important laws for preventing and controlling air pollution in India.

Here are some of the key provisions of the Air (Prevention and Control of Pollution) Act, 1981:

- The Act defines air pollution as the presence of any air pollutant in the atmosphere in such concentration as may be or tend to be injurious to human health or to the environment.
- The Act prohibits the emission of any air pollutant from any source without a permit from the SPCB.
- The SPCBs can take measures to prevent and control air pollution, such as issuing directions to industries and other polluters, and taking legal action against them.
- The Act provides for the establishment of laboratories to test the quality of air.
- The Act provides for the establishment of an air quality monitoring network.

- The Act provides for the education and training of people in air pollution control.

(v) The Environment (Protection) Act, 1986:

The Environment (Protection) Act, 1986 is an Act of the Parliament of India enacted to provide for the protection and improvement of the environment and for matters connected therewith. It is one of the most important environmental laws in India.

The Act establishes the Ministry of Environment, Forest and Climate Change (MoEFCC) and the Central Pollution Control Board (CPCB) to oversee the implementation of the Act. The MoEFCC is responsible for formulating national environmental policies and for coordinating the activities of the CPCB and other government agencies. The CPCB is responsible for setting standards for air, water, and noise pollution, and for monitoring and enforcing compliance with these standards.

The Act prohibits the discharge of any environmental pollutant in excess of prescribed standards. It also prohibits the handling of hazardous substances without a permit from the CPCB. The Act also provides for the establishment of environmental laboratories and for the education and training of people in environmental protection.

The Act has been amended several times since it was enacted, and it is currently one of the most important laws for protecting the environment in India.

Here are some of the key provisions of the Environment (Protection) Act, 1986:

- The Act defines the environment as the totality of the surroundings of a human being, including the physical, chemical, biological, social, economic and cultural conditions that influence his life and well-being.

- The Act prohibits the discharge of any environmental pollutant in excess of prescribed standards.
- The Act prohibits the handling of hazardous substances without a permit from the CPCB.
- The Act provides for the establishment of environmental laboratories and for the education and training of people in environmental protection.
- The Act provides for the punishment of persons who violate the provisions of the Act.

(vi). The National Green Tribunal Act, 2010

The National Green Tribunal Act, 2010 is an Act of the Parliament of India that establishes the National Green Tribunal (NGT) for the effective and expeditious disposal of cases relating to environmental protection and conservation of forests and other natural resources.

The NGT is a specialized tribunal with jurisdiction over all matters relating to environmental protection and conservation of forests and other natural resources. It has the power to hear and decide applications and appeals relating to environmental issues, such as air pollution, water pollution, noise pollution, and deforestation. The NGT can also award compensation for damages caused to the environment.

The NGT is composed of a Chairperson and two judicial members, who are appointed by the President of India. The Chairperson and judicial members must be persons who have had a distinguished career in the field of law or environmental science. The NGT also has two expert members, who are appointed by the Central Government. The expert members must be persons who have specialized knowledge or experience in environmental matters.

The NGT has its headquarters in New Delhi, and it has benches in Bhopal, Pune, Kolkata, and Chennai. The NGT can also sit at any other place in India as it may deem fit.

The NGT is a significant step towards the protection of the environment in India. It provides a forum for the speedy resolution of environmental disputes, and it can help to ensure that environmental laws are enforced effectively.

Here are some of the key provisions of the National Green Tribunal Act, 2010:

- The Act establishes the National Green Tribunal (NGT) for the effective and expeditious disposal of cases relating to environmental protection and conservation of forests and other natural resources.
- The NGT has jurisdiction over all matters relating to environmental protection and conservation of forests and other natural resources.
- The NGT can hear and decide applications and appeals relating to environmental issues, such as air pollution, water pollution, noise pollution, and deforestation.
- The NGT can also award compensation for damages caused to the environment.
- The NGT is composed of a Chairperson and two judicial members, who are appointed by the President of India.
- The NGT also has two expert members, who are appointed by the Central Government.
- The NGT has its headquarters in New Delhi, and it has benches in Bhopal, Pune, Kolkata, and Chennai.
- The NGT can also sit at any other place in India as it may deem fit.

The National Green Tribunal Act, 2010 is a landmark legislation that has the potential to make a significant contribution to the protection of the environment in India. By providing a forum for the speedy resolution of environmental disputes, and by empowering the NGT to take effective action against environmental polluters, the Act can help to ensure that India's natural resources are protected for future generations.

(vii). Hazardous Waste Management Regulation

Hazardous waste management regulation is a set of laws and regulations that govern the generation, transportation, treatment, storage, and disposal of hazardous waste. The goal of hazardous waste management regulation is to protect human health and the environment from the harmful effects of hazardous waste.

In India, the hazardous waste management regulation is governed by the Hazardous Wastes (Management and Handling) Rules, 2000. These rules were issued by the Ministry of Environment, Forest and Climate Change (MoEFCC) under the Environment (Protection) Act, 1986.

The Hazardous Wastes (Management and Handling) Rules, 2000 define hazardous waste as any waste that exhibits any of the following characteristics:

- Ignitability: The ability to catch fire easily.
- Corrosivity: The ability to cause damage to living tissue or metal.
- Reactivity: The ability to react with other substances to produce dangerous or unstable materials.
- Toxicity: The ability to cause harm to human health or the environment.

The Hazardous Wastes (Management and Handling) Rules, 2000 require that all generators of hazardous waste obtain a permit from the State Pollution Control Board (SPCB) before generating, transporting, treating, storing, or disposing of hazardous waste. The SPCB will issue a permit only if the generator can demonstrate that they have the necessary facilities and procedures in place to safely manage hazardous waste.

B. Stages of Becoming An Ecologically Sustainable Organization

There are many stages of becoming an ecologically sustainable organization. Here are some of the key stages:

1. **Pre-compliance:** This is the stage where the organization is not yet in compliance with environmental regulations. However, it is taking steps to become compliant, such as conducting an environmental audit and developing an environmental management plan.
2. **Compliance:** This is the stage where the organization is in compliance with environmental regulations. It is continuously monitoring its environmental performance and making improvements where necessary.
3. **Beyond compliance:** This is the stage where the organization is going beyond what is required by environmental regulations. It is taking steps to reduce its environmental impact, such as investing in renewable energy and energy efficiency measures.
4. **Leadership:** This is the stage where the organization is a leader in environmental sustainability. It is sharing its knowledge and expertise with other organizations and helping to promote environmental protection.

The specific stages that an organization goes through will vary depending on its size, industry, and location. However, all organizations can take steps to become more ecologically sustainable.

Here are some of the things that organizations can do to become more ecologically sustainable:

- Conduct an environmental audit to identify their environmental impacts.
- Develop an environmental management plan to reduce their environmental impacts.
- Invest in renewable energy and energy efficiency measures.
- Reduce their waste production and recycle and compost materials.
- Use sustainable materials and practices in their operations.
- Educate their employees about environmental sustainability.
- Share their knowledge and expertise with other organizations.
- Help to promote environmental protection.

By taking these steps, organizations can make a positive contribution to the environment and help to build a more sustainable future.

4.5.1. Sustainable Development

Sustainable development is a broad term that encompasses many different concepts. It is generally understood to mean development that meets the needs of the present without compromising the ability of future generations to meet their own needs. This means that sustainable development must balance economic development, environmental protection, and social equity.

The concept of sustainable development was first popularized in the 1987 Brundtland Report, which was commissioned by the United

Nations. The report defined sustainable development as "development that meets the needs of the present without compromising the ability of future generations to meet their own needs."

A. Application of Environmental Sustainability

Environmental sustainability is the practice of meeting the needs of the present without compromising the ability of future generations to meet their own needs. It is a broad concept that can be applied to many different areas of life, including:

(i). Sustainable Agriculture:

Sustainable agriculture is farming in a way that meets the needs of the present without compromising the ability of future generations to meet their own needs. It is a system of agriculture that seeks to balance three main objectives: environmental health, economic profitability, and social and economic equity.

There are many different practices that can be used to achieve sustainable agriculture. Some of the most common include:

- **Crop rotation:** This is the practice of rotating different crops through the same field each year. This helps to prevent soil depletion and the buildup of pests and diseases.
- **Cover cropping:** This is the practice of planting cover crops, such as legumes or grasses, in the off-season. Cover crops help to improve soil health and reduce erosion.
- **Integrated pest management:** This is a system of pest control that uses a variety of methods, such as crop rotation, biological controls, and natural pesticides, to reduce the use of synthetic pesticides.

(ii). Sustainable forestry

Sustainable forestry is the practice of managing forests to meet the needs of the present without compromising the ability of future generations to meet their own needs. It is a system of forestry that seeks to balance three main objectives: environmental health, economic profitability, and social and economic equity.

Some of the key principles of sustainable forestry include:

- **Protecting biodiversity:** Sustainable forestry seeks to maintain the diversity of plant and animal life in forests. This is important for a number of reasons, including the provision of ecosystem services such as pollination and pest control, and the resilience of forests to pests and diseases.
- **Conserving water resources:** Forests play an important role in the water cycle, by storing water and releasing it slowly into streams and rivers. Sustainable forestry practices help to conserve water resources by reducing erosion and promoting infiltration of water into the soil.
- **Minimizing soil disturbance:** Sustainable forestry practices minimize soil disturbance, which helps to protect the soil from erosion and degradation. This is important for maintaining the productivity of forests and preventing the release of greenhouse gases into the atmosphere.

Environmental Limits

Environmental limits are the boundaries beyond which exploitation of a natural resource will have significant deleterious effects. Natural resources include land, water, air and associated living systems that comprise the biosphere.

There are many different environmental limits that have been identified. Some of the most important include:

- Climate change: The Earth's climate is changing at an unprecedented rate due to human activities, such as the burning of fossil fuels. This is causing a number of problems, such as rising sea levels, more extreme weather events, and changes in agricultural yields.
- Ocean acidification: The oceans are absorbing carbon dioxide from the atmosphere, which is making them more acidic. This is harming marine life, such as coral reefs and shellfish.
- Stratospheric ozone depletion: The ozone layer protects us from harmful ultraviolet radiation from the sun. However, ozone-depleting substances, such as chlorofluorocarbons (CFCs), have been released into the atmosphere, and this has caused a hole in the ozone layer.
- Nitrogen and phosphorus losses: Nitrogen and phosphorus are essential nutrients for plants, but excessive amounts can pollute waterways and cause algal blooms.
- Atmospheric aerosol loading: Aerosols are tiny particles suspended in the atmosphere. They can have a number of negative effects, such as reducing visibility and harming human health.
- Freshwater use: Water is a finite resource, and its use is increasing due to population growth and economic development. This is putting a strain on freshwater resources, and it is leading to water scarcity in some parts of the world.

Sustainable Consumption

Sustainable consumption is the use of products and services that meet our needs and improve our quality of life, while minimizing the negative impacts on the environment and people. It is about doing more and better with less.

Sustainable consumption is important because it can help to reduce our impact on the environment, conserve resources, and create a more just and equitable society. It is also about making choices that are good for our own health and well-being.

Here are some of the benefits of sustainable consumption:

- It can help to reduce pollution and greenhouse gas emissions.
- It can conserve natural resources, such as water and energy.
- It can create jobs in the clean energy and recycling industries.
- It can improve public health by reducing exposure to toxins.
- It can help to build a more just and equitable society by ensuring that everyone has access to the resources they need.

There are many things that we can do to practice sustainable consumption. Here are a few ideas:

- **Be mindful of our choices.** When we buy something, we should think about the environmental and social impacts of our purchase.
- **Choose products that are made sustainably.** There are many products available that are made from recycled materials, that are energy-efficient, or that are produced in an environmentally friendly way.
- **Reduce, reuse, and recycle.** We can reduce our environmental impact by reducing the amount of stuff we consume, reusing items whenever possible, and recycling materials when we can't reuse them.
- **Support sustainable businesses.** There are many businesses that are committed to sustainable practices. By supporting these businesses, we can help to create a more sustainable economy.

Sustainable consumption is not always easy, but it is important. By making small changes in our everyday lives, we can make a big difference for the planet.

4.6. Principles of Environmental Ethics:

There are many different principles of environmental ethics, but some of the most important ones include:

- **Respect for nature:** This principle holds that nature has intrinsic value, or value in and of itself, and should be respected for its own sake.
- **Sustainability:** This principle holds that we should use natural resources in a way that ensures their long-term availability.
- **Interdependence:** This principle holds that humans and other living things are interdependent, and that we have a responsibility to care for the environment for the sake of future generations.
- **Equity:** This principle holds that we should strive for a just and equitable distribution of environmental resources, both within and between generations.
- **Precautionary principle:** This principle holds that we should err on the side of caution when it comes to environmental risks, and take action to prevent harm even if the evidence is not conclusive.
- **Right to know:** This principle holds that people have a right to access information about environmental risks.
- **Right to participate:** This principle holds that people have a right to participate in decision-making about environmental issues.
- **Solidarity:** This principle holds that we have a responsibility

to help others, especially those who are most affected by environmental degradation.

- **Reparation:** This principle holds that we have a responsibility to repair the damage we have caused to the environment.

- **Sustainable development:** This principle holds that we can achieve economic development without compromising the environment.

- **Intergenerational equity:** This principle holds that we have a responsibility to ensure that future generations inherit a healthy environment.

- **Cosmopolitan ethics:** This principle holds that we have a responsibility to care for the environment, regardless of national borders.

These are just some of the many principles of environmental ethics. The specific principles that are most important will vary depending on the specific context. However, all of these principles are important for promoting a more sustainable and ethical relationship between humans and the environment.

Ambient Ethics

Ambient ethics is a branch of ethics that deals with the ethical implications of ambient intelligence, which is a type of technology that creates a seamless and invisible environment that adapts to the needs of the user. Ambient intelligence technologies are often used in smart homes, wearable devices, and other everyday objects.

There are several forms of ambient ethics, including:

- **Privacy:** Ambient intelligence technologies often collect and store data about users, which raises privacy concerns. For example, a smart home could collect data about the user's movements, activities, and interactions with devices. This data could be used to track the user's habits, preferences, and even mental state.

- **Security:** Ambient intelligence technologies are also vulnerable to security risks. For example, a hacker could gain access to a smart home's network and control the devices in the home. This could be used to steal personal information, cause damage, or even harm the inhabitants of the home.

- **Discrimination:** Ambient intelligence technologies could be used to discriminate against certain groups of people. For example, a facial recognition system could be used to deny access to a service to people of a certain race or ethnicity.

- **Fairness:** Ambient intelligence technologies should be designed in a way that is fair to all users. This means that the technologies should not discriminate against any group of people and should not be used to exploit or harm anyone.

- **Transparency:** Users should be aware of how ambient intelligence technologies work and how their data is being collected and used. This means that companies should provide clear and transparent privacy policies and should not collect or use data without the user's consent.

These are just some of the forms of ambient ethics. As ambient intelligence technologies become more widespread, it is important to consider the ethical implications of these technologies and to develop ethical guidelines for their use.

4.6.1. Difference Between Consumer and Consumerism

Consumerism and customers are often used interchangeably, but they have different meanings. A **consumer** is someone who buys goods and services from a business. They are the end-user of the product or service. **Consumerism** is a social and economic system that encourages the acquisition of goods and services. It is often characterized by an emphasis on material possessions and a desire for the latest and greatest products.

Here are some key differences between consumerism and customers:

- **Focus:** Consumers focus on meeting their needs and wants, while consumerism focuses on the acquisition of material possessions.
- **Motivation:** Consumers are motivated by a variety of factors, including the need for products and services, the desire for convenience, and the pursuit of happiness. Consumerism is motivated by a desire for social status and a sense of belonging.
- **Impact:** Consumers can have a positive impact on the economy by stimulating demand for goods and services. Consumerism can have a negative impact on the economy by leading to overconsumption and debt.
- **Sustainability:** Consumers can make choices that are more sustainable by buying products that are made from recycled materials or that are energy-efficient. Consumerism can have a negative impact on the environment by leading to the depletion of natural resources and pollution.
- **Society:** Consumers can contribute to a more just and equitable society by buying products that are made ethically and that support sustainable practices. Consumerism can lead to social inequality by creating a culture of materialism and conspicuous consumption.

4.6.2. Customer Idioms

Some customer idioms are:

- **The customer is always right:** This idiom means that businesses should always put the needs of their customers first.
- **The customer has the power:** This idiom means that customers have the power to choose where to spend their money. Businesses should be aware of this and strive to provide good customer service.
- **Losing a customer is like losing money twice:** This idiom means that it is more expensive to acquire a new customer than it is to keep an existing customer. Businesses should focus on keeping their existing customers happy.
- **A happy customer is a repeat customer:** This idiom means that customers who are happy with their experience with a business are more likely to do business with that business again. Businesses should focus on providing good customer service to create happy customers.
- **Word of mouth is powerful:** This idiom means that positive word-of-mouth from satisfied customers can be very effective in attracting new customers. Businesses should focus on providing good customer service to create satisfied customers who will spread positive word-of-mouth.

These are just a few examples of customer idioms. There are many others, and the meaning of each idiom can vary depending on the context.

4.6.3. Types of Consumer

There are many different types of consumers, but some of the most common include:

- **Loyal customers:** These are customers who regularly buy from the same businesses and are less likely to switch brands. They are valuable to businesses because they are more likely to spend money and recommend the business to others.
- **Impulse buyers:** These are customers who buy things without much thought or planning. They are often attracted to sales and promotions.
- **Bargain hunters:** These are customers who are always looking for the best deals. They are often willing to wait for sales or to shop around for the best price.
- **Brand-loyal customers:** These are customers who are loyal to certain brands. They are often willing to pay more for a brand that they trust.
- **Influencers:** These are customers who have a large following on social media. They can be very influential in shaping the buying decisions of their followers.
- **Emotional buyers:** These are customers who buy things based on their emotions, rather than their rational thinking. They are often attracted to products that make them feel good or that make them feel like they belong.
- **Status seekers:** These are customers who buy things to show off their social status. They are often attracted to luxury brands and products.
- **Eco-conscious consumers:** These are customers who are concerned about the environment. They are often willing to pay more for products that are sustainable or environmentally friendly.
- **Experience seekers:** These are customers who are looking for new and exciting experiences. They are often willing to try new products and services.

These are just some of the many different types of consumers. Businesses can target their marketing and sales efforts to different types of consumers to be more effective.

4.7. Government Regulation Agencies for Consumer Protection and Protecting Consumer Privacy Online:

government regulation agencies for consumer protection and protecting consumer privacy online:

Consumer protection is the safeguarding of consumers' rights and interests in the marketplace. It includes protecting consumers from unfair, deceptive, and fraudulent practices, as well as protecting their privacy.

There are many government regulation agencies that are responsible for consumer protection. These agencies have different jurisdictions, but they all work to ensure that consumers are treated fairly and that their privacy is protected.

Some of the most important government regulation agencies for consumer protection include:

- **Federal Trade Commission (FTC):** The FTC is the primary consumer protection agency in the United States. It enforces laws that protect consumers from unfair, deceptive, and fraudulent practices. The FTC also has authority to protect consumer privacy online.
- **Consumer Financial Protection Bureau (CFPB):** The CFPB is a consumer protection agency that was created in 2010. It enforces laws that protect consumers in the financial marketplace, including credit cards, mortgages, and payday loans. The CFPB also has authority to protect consumer privacy online.

- **Securities and Exchange Commission (SEC):** The SEC is a federal agency that regulates the securities markets. It enforces laws that protect investors from fraud and abuse. The SEC also has authority to protect consumer privacy online, but its focus is on protecting investors from fraud and abuse.

- **Health Insurance Portability and Accountability Act (HIPAA):** HIPAA is a federal law that protects the privacy of health information. It applies to health care providers, health plans, and health care clearinghouses. HIPAA requires these entities to take steps to protect the privacy of patient information, including using strong security measures and giving patients control over their information.

- **Children's Online Privacy Protection Act (COPPA):** COPPA is a federal law that protects the privacy of children under the age of 13. It applies to websites and online services that collect personal information from children. COPPA requires these entities to obtain parental consent before collecting or using personal information from children.

- These are just some of the most important government regulation agencies that protect consumer privacy online. There are many other agencies that have jurisdiction over specific industries or types of data.

- The FTC is the primary agency responsible for enforcing laws that protect consumer privacy online. The FTC has issued a number of guidelines and regulations that businesses must follow to protect consumer privacy. For example, the FTC requires businesses to obtain consumers' consent before collecting or using their personal information. The FTC also requires businesses to take steps to protect the security of consumers' personal information.

- The CFPB also has authority to protect consumer privacy

online. The CFPB enforces laws that protect consumers in the financial marketplace, including credit cards, mortgages, and payday loans. The CFPB has issued a number of regulations that businesses must follow to protect consumer privacy in the financial marketplace. For example, the CFPB requires businesses to provide consumers with clear and concise information about how their personal information will be used.

- The SEC also has some authority to protect consumer privacy online. The SEC enforces laws that protect investors from fraud and abuse. The SEC has issued a number of guidance documents that businesses should follow to protect consumer privacy online. For example, the SEC guidance document on cybersecurity recommends that businesses take steps to protect the security of their computer systems and networks.

- HIPAA is a federal law that protects the privacy of health information. HIPAA applies to health care providers, health plans, and health care clearinghouses. HIPAA requires these entities to take steps to protect the privacy of patient information, including using strong security measures and giving patients control over their information.

- COPPA is a federal law that protects the privacy of children under the age of 13. COPPA applies to websites and online services that collect personal information from children. COPPA requires these entities to obtain parental consent before collecting or using personal information from children.

About Author

Surjeet Kumar is engaged in teaching for more than a decade and writer by passion. He believes books are the mode of expressions that bind the vision and emotions in wonderful reality. He have written more than ten poetry books on numerous topics such as emotional, empathy, thrilling, inspirational, loneliness, reflection, introspection and many more since his school days. He is grateful to his readers and their opinions which support him to enhance his capacity in writing. Now, in his research journey he is is trying to add chapters of his books to the academic curriculum.

About the Author

Surjeet Kumar is Assistant Professor by profession and writer by passion. He believes, poems are the mode of expressions that bind the vision and emotions in wonderful phrases. Poems have an ability to decorate ambiance along with infusing strengths among people whenever s/he does not feel comfortable. He has been fond of writing on numerous topics such as love, empathy, thrilling, inspirational, loneliness, reflection, introspection and many more since his school days. He would like to amaze his readers by his writing style on contemporary topics. He is grateful to his readers and their opinions which support him to enhance his capacity in writing poems.